NATURAL STAIN REMOVAL SECRETS

NATURAL STAIN REMOVAL SECRETS

Powerful, safe techniques for removing stubborn stains from anything

DEBORAH L. MARTIN

This edition published in 2010 by
CRESTLINE
a division of BOOK SALES, INC.
276 Fifth Avenue Suite 206
New York, New York 10001
USA

First published in the USA in 2007 by
Fair Winds Press, a member of
Quayside Publishing Group
100 Cummings Center
Suite 406-L
Beverly, MA 01915

11 10   1 2 3 4 5

ISBN-13: 978-0-7858-2643-9
ISBN-10: 0-7858-2643-2

Library of Congress Cataloging-in-Publication Data available

Book design by Laura McFadden

Printed and bound in China

CONTENTS

INTRODUCTION

Don't Let a Spill Put You on the Spot

THE MOMENTS RIGHT AFTER A SPILL are often chaotic. As the stain-in-the-making settles on its target surface, the decisions you make and the actions you take while "on the spot" can determine whether the spill is a quickly forgotten "oops" or a lingering reminder of what went wrong.

This book is intended to help you deal with the spills and spots that life throws your way. Starting with a description of stain-removal dos and don'ts, it offers tips and techniques for using safe and natural solutions to make the least of stains. You'll also find a list of stain-removal materials you may already have at home, along with a few others that you may wish to add to your cleaning cupboard.

Sorting Out the Stains

Stains fall into a few general types, and similar treatments can be applied to the stains of a type with reasonable success. The most common stain types are:

- **Protein stains** (animal-related: blood, eggs, bodily fluids, etc.)
- **Tannin stains** (plant-related: coffee, tea, fruit, wine, etc.)
- **Greasy/oily stains** (automotive grease and oil, cooking grease and oil, lotions, creams, etc.)
- **Dye stains** (colors bled from fabrics, felt-tip ink, food coloring, etc.)
- **Combination and other kinds of stains** (greasy dirt, adhesives, minerals, paints, physical damage, etc.)

Following the sections on stain-fighting tools, a chapter for each type of stain will help you recall the proper treatments for that category. The stains in each category are listed alphabetically, with stain removal solutions suggested in order from the safest to the harshest.

You May Need to "Tough it Out"

For some stains, the removal method of last resort involves a harsh chemical that falls outside the realm of what would generally be called "natural." This is not to suggest that natural stain-removal techniques can't resolve the vast majority of stains. Rather, it acknowledges that most successful stain removal involves chemistry. Effective stain removal happens when the staining agent forms a solution with the treatment you use on it and can be flushed out (or off) of whatever it is staining. In other words, stain treatments are meant to dissolve staining agents.

Any high school chemistry teacher will tell you that "like dissolves like." Thus, water is a good solvent for most water-based stains, while oil-based stains respond better to oily treatments (followed by detergents to get rid of the oil residue). Following this chemistry lesson to its "natural" conclusion, you can see that stains that are caused by complex combinations of chemicals—some dyes, inks, paints, etc.— require harsh chemicals or solvents to dissolve them.

When you encounter a tough stain—red nail polish on the upholstery, for example—how far you choose to go in treating it is up to you. If your upholstery fabric will tolerate it, nail-polish remover is ultimately your best bet for making the stain go away. You can do this treatment yourself, using the smallest amount of polish remover necessary to do the job, taking all proper precautions to protect yourself while you work, and disposing of soiled cleaning cloths in an environmentally responsible way. Or, you may opt for professional treatment, with the understanding that the removal process is unlikely to be natural. It's up to you to decide your level of tolerance for using a moderately or highly toxic product or treatment to remove a stain, or simply living with it.

Why "Go Natural" for Stain Removal?

THERE ARE MANY REASONS, for choosing a natural approach to stain removal. Foremost among them may be safeguarding your family's health. Not all chemical cleaners are inherently bad or dangerous, nor are all "natural" cleaning materials safe and risk-free. But many harsh cleaning products come with such a long list of warnings that it only makes sense to avoid exposure to them as much as possible. Chemical sensitivity is a growing concern and, for sensitive individuals especially, avoiding exposure to toxic chemicals may be a medical necessity.

Natural stain removal can save you money, too. It replaces an arsenal of chemicals with knowledge, common sense, and a few basic cleaning products, many of which you may already have in your home. A number of these household cleansers are inexpensive, especially compared to commercial cleaning products. Baking soda, for example, is an excellent and safe abrasive cleanser that can be used to gently scour spots off many surfaces; it's also useful for absorbing liquid spills and neutralizing acid stains. You can buy a large box of baking soda for the same price as (or less than) the smallest-sized bottle of a popular liquid scrubbing product—and the baking soda has more uses and none of the harsh chemical additives found in the commercial product!

It's also more convenient to use common household products. You can quickly reach for the baking soda, grab the salt shaker, or stir some white vinegar into water instead of running to the store for a stain-removal product, or spending part of your shopping excursion pondering the differences between products.

Protecting the environment is another good reason for taking a natural approach to stain removal. Many of the cleaning products in use twenty to thirty years ago are no longer on the market. Why? Because we discovered that they harmed the environment, often in ways that only became apparent after years of use. Laundry detergents used to contain phosphates: chemicals added to whiten and brighten fabrics. As the use of products containing phosphates grew, and as more households produced phosphate-laden rinse water that ended up in rivers and streams, we discovered there was a downside to all that whitening and brightening. The phosphates fertilized algae, and the algae grew until it choked the life out of many waterways. It took years to discover the connection between phosphates in detergents and clogged, stagnant rivers, and many more years for those waterways to recover once we stopped pouring phosphates into them.

There are many other examples of products once believed to be safe that have turned out to pose risks to the environment (and to human health). And although not all natural stain-removal products are entirely harmless, as a group they pose far fewer hazards to the environment than do the complex chemical compounds that make up most commercial cleaning products.

Removing stains naturally is both easier and harder than reaching for a bottle of the latest commercially available stain-busting concoction. It's easier because you can treat spills quickly and simply, thus stopping them from ever becoming stains. It's harder in that there is no "magic bullet" for difficult stains; no all-purpose, safe-chemical creation to answer the wide array of substances that seem intent upon leaving their marks on our clothing, carpets, floors, and furnishings.

Treat Stains with Safety, Too

A few words of caution: Tough stains sometimes call for tough treatments, and even common household products and natural materials may require careful handling to safeguard your health. The designation "natural" doesn't always mean "so safe you can eat/drink/breathe/apply it" without risking harm. Throughout this book, you'll find stain treatments listed in order from least toxic to most; don't bring out the big guns until you've tried the simpler, safer solutions. If you must use harsher products to handle difficult or set-in stains, read the label and follow all the recommended precautions for a particular stain-fighter. Ultimately, you'll have to decide if removing the stain is worth the potential risks associated with using tougher treatments.

In general, when working with household chemicals—even natural ones—observe the following safety guidelines:

🌿 **Work in a well-ventilated area.** This is especially important when working with solvents.

🌿 **Protect your hands with rubber gloves.** Even mild soaps and detergents will dry out your hands and nails with repeated exposure.

- **Store all household chemicals in clearly labeled containers** in locked cupboards where children and pets cannot reach them.

- **Label homemade stain-removal solutions** and store them securely with your cleaning products.

- **Do not store homemade stain-removal mixtures** in food or beverage containers.

- **Never mix household products without specific knowledge of the results.** In some cases, combining chemicals can produce dangerous reactions and toxic by-products.

- **Keep the phone number for your regional poison control center** near your phone, along with other emergency numbers.

Dos and Don'ts for Successful Stain Removal

I T MAY SEEM CONTRADICTORY, but speed and patience are the keys to stain-removal success. When a spill happens, you need to act quickly to minimize the damage, but you also need to appropriately and patiently apply the treatment that's most likely to prevent the spill from becoming a stain. In short, you need to hurry up and take your time. Don't worry, it's not as impossible as it sounds.

If the old saying about never getting a second chance to make a first impression is true, then the stain-treatment corollary should be, "You never get a second chance to remove a first impression." Of course, that's not entirely accurate, as you'll find a number of second- and third-chance treatment options throughout this book, but first treatments, like first impressions, always make—or in this case, reduce—the biggest mark. The folloing are some key dos and don'ts to first-treatment stain removal:

- ❦ **Do use a light touch.** It's tempting to put some muscle into your stain-removal efforts, trying to rub and scrub at a spot until it's driven away by force. A heavy hand on all but the sturdiest surfaces, however, can cause damage that remains even after the stain is gone. Rubbing fabrics (including carpet and uphol-stery) frays the fibers and makes them "fuzz up." You may remove the stain, but you'll likely leave behind damaged fibers that stand out nearly as much. Such fibers are not only prone to collecting dirt, but they're also likely to wear out more quickly and make a hole.

☙ **Do treat stains when they're fresh.** Don't wait until laundry day rolls around. Nearly every stain you encounter is easiest to remove when it's fresh. In fact, much of the success of natural removal methods involves keeping spills from ever becoming stains by cleaning them up as quickly as possible and using solutions that dissolve them away instead of setting them in.

☙ **Do keep dry spills dry and wet spills wet.** Imagine shampooing a heavily soiled carpet without first vacuuming it thoroughly to pick up the loose dirt. In a very short time, you'd have a wet, muddy mess, and the cleaning solution would only serve to drive the soil deeper into the carpet fibers. Don't put a drop of liquid on a dry spill (or mark) until you've vacuumed, shaken, brushed, or blown away every particle you possibly can. Then—and only then—should you consider using a liquid treatment to remove any dye transfer.

As for keeping wet stains wet, remember that like dissolves like. If liquid carried the stain onto the surface, it's likely that liquid will carry it off. Drying a liquid stain only takes away its transportation and leaves the dyes and solid materials to cling tightly to your stuff.

☙ **Don't rub it in.** When a staining agent gets on an item, the goal is to remove it, ideally before it leaves a stain. Avoid the urge to wipe, rub, or otherwise press on solid and semi-solid spills; you'll only force them into the surface they're trying to stain, and you'll be left trying to force them back out. With a lifting motion, wield a spoon, a dull knife, a spatula, or even a credit card to carefully scrape the spill off your stuff. Whatever the stain is made of, it'll be so much easier to remove completely if you keep it superficial.

☙ **Do work in good lighting.** This is mostly a laundry room recommendation. If the lighting in your laundry room is inadequate or distorts color perceptions, you're likely to miss seeing stains that have been waiting for laundry-day treatment, and you'll have a hard time determining whether your stain-treatment efforts are successful or not. Install bulbs that deliver natural-looking light. Add a light fixture or a lamp to chase away shadows that can hide stains from clear view. When treating a stain that's fallen outside the reach of your home's lighting fixtures (e.g., a carpet stain in the corner of a room) temporarily position a lamp at the location of the stain.

🌿 **Do know your garments.** When faced with a spill and potential stain, ask yourself these questions: What solution will dissolve the staining agent? What solutions are safe to apply?

It does little good to remove a stain from your favorite wool sweater if the ammonia solution you use irreparably damages the fibers. Fortunately, knowing the fiber content of garments is usually as easy as checking the content label. Most garments also have a fabric care label that tells you the recommended water temperature for washing, whether it's safe to use bleach, and how to safely dry the garment.

❧ **Do bring in "back-up."** When treating stains on fabrics, always place an absorbent pad under the stain to soak up the staining material and soiled cleaning solution as it moves out of the fabric. If you don't make a habit of doing this, you run the risk of removing a stain from one part of a garment and sponging it onto another. Refold or replace the pad frequently to keep the stain from reapplying to the surface you're treating. Clean, light-colored towels and washcloths work very well for this, as do cloth diapers. Nearly any absorbent cloth will do, as long as it's clean and colorfast. You can also make a pad with several layers of white paper toweling. It makes sense to keep a supply of clean, light-colored cloths or rags on hand for this purpose.

🌿 **Do get under the stain.** It's not always possible, but when you can, work from the underside of a spot on fabric. Assuming the stain landed on the outside of the fabric, treating it from the underside helps to push it off the surface instead of pushing it through. This lessens the chance that the stain will settle into the fabric's fibers and also reduces the likelihood that you'll abrade the surface of the fabric by rubbing the stained area. Simply lay your garment stain side down on a cloth pad, and treat from beneath.

🌿 **Do clean out the cleanser.** When you're through applying stain treatments to carpet or upholstery, be sure to rinse and blot the area with clear water. Otherwise, the residue left by the cleaning solution will attract soil to the treated area, and instead of a stain, you'll have a dirty spot. You may not need to rinse stain treatments out of washable items if the next step in the process is laundering. When switching from one treatment to another without laundering in between, it is important to rinse out the first treatment solution completely to avoid combining incompatible household chemicals that could release dangerous fumes or damage the item you're treating.

Support the Home Team

When a spot or spill lands on your carpet, your sofa, your flooring, or your kitchen countertop, it's essential to know the appropriate cleaning methods for that surface. Can you use water, or does it require a special cleaning product? Will using an abrasive cleaner damage the finish? What can you use to get out the stain without fading the color? Since doing the wrong thing—using a cleaning product or method that goes against the manufacturer's recommenda- tions, for example—can void your warrantee and make the problem worse, it really pays to know what to do and what to avoid when a spill happens.

Here's the key: Don't rely on your memory to know what to do. When you've spent weeks researching kitchen flooring and even longer shopping and arranging installation for it, you may feel that you know that surface so completely that you'll always know exactly how to care for it and clean it. Ditto for your

🍂 **Do meet the maker.** If the stain in question was caused by a product, you may find that the best treatment recommendations come from the product's manufacturer. Start with the product label—it may

leather couch, your Oriental rug, and the paint on your bathroom walls. The sad truth, however, is that spending a lot of money on something does not guarantee that you'll remember, in a few months or a few years, the specific care instructions recommended for that surface or item. Saving yourself from frustration is extremely simple: Keep a file (or two—one physical and one electronic) of the stuff in your house and keep it handy. Make sure it includes warrantee information and cleaning/care instructions. A simple expandable file folder works great. When you buy, install, or paint anything, toss the associated documents into the folder, so that when a stain crops up, you know where to look. If you keep an up-to-date computer file, include links to manufacturers' websites, along with product information, so you can get the latest on recalls, as well as the right care guidelines. If you don't have such a file already, don't wait for a spill or stain to prompt you to start one. It's tempting to think you'll remember how to handle cleanups on your household furnishings, but time has a way of dimming those memories—and the stress of a stain can wipe them away completely.

tell you everything you need to know. In the absence of that information on the label (or in the absence of a label), visit the manufacturer's website, or give its customer service department a call. Responsible manufacturers of products with a high potential for causing stains (think glues, paints, and children's art supplies) have become quite sophisticated at providing this type of information.

❧ **Do ask the big question:** Treat it or toss it? Some stains are difficult or impossible to remove. In those cases, you have to decide how much time and effort you want to invest in treating the stain. Oftentimes, the stain's location makes the difference. Is it in the middle of your two-year-old living room carpet, or on the front of your twenty-year-old concert T-shirt? Although you may regret the loss of the shirt (or decide that a stain simply adds to its "vintage" look), it won't cost hundreds of dollars to replace it (or require you to hide it with a piece of furniture) if it's irretrievably stained.

🌿 **Do consider seeking professional help.** A stain that's relatively easy to remove from washable fabric may require a much different treatment on a dryclean-only garment. Stains on upholstery, too, may require professional treatment, especially if the upholstery fabric is not meant to be cleaned with water.

🌿 **Don't give up.** This one's simple: Tough stains may require repeat treatment, and you may have to vary your tactics until you find the right solution.

🌿 **Don't spread it around.** It's all too easy, in the excitement of a spill, to accidentally drip spilled liquid from blotting cloths across the carpet or to smear the spaghetti sauce beyond the margins of the original spot. As you scrape, lift, and/or blot, work from the outer edges of a stain inward to the center to avoid making a bigger stain. Do the same when you apply water or cleaning solutions—your goal is to make the stain smaller, then to make it vanish entirely. Don't work against yourself.

Take a Thoughtful Approach to Solving Stains

When a stain happens, it's tempting to toss on a treatment and get back to whatever you were doing. But that can be a recipe for disaster (and lead to lasting damage), especially if you're trying a new stain-removal method on a visible location—the lapel of your favorite jacket or the middle of the living room rug, for example. Acting in haste can do more harm than good if the treatment you apply sets the stain instead of removing it, or takes out the color in your carpet along with the stain. In most staining situations, what you should do quickly is contain and soak up liquid spills and gently scrape up solid and

Test Before You Treat

In the panic of trying to treat a new stain, patience can be difficult to come by. But it makes sense to try out any new stain solution in a hidden or inconspicuous spot first. After all, if the item is worth the effort to remove the stain, it's also worth the effort to ensure that the treatment won't inflict its own damage. Here's how to test:

1. Choose a secure location. On clothing, consider the hem or seam allowances (where the face of the fabric is turned under or to the inside of the garment), or beneath a flap covering a zipper. Choose locations under the cushions of upholstered furniture. For carpets or flooring, use the floor inside a closet, under a piece of furniture, or in the corner behind a door.

2. Put several drops of the cleaning solution on the test site.

3. Moisten a clean white cloth with water, and press it against the test spot for one minute.

4. Check the cloth for any signs of color transferring from the surface; check the surface for signs of color changes or other damage. If any negative effects are evident, try a different stain-treatment method. Clear the removal solution from the test area using the same method recommended when applying it to stains.

semi-solid materials. While you're doing that, consider these three questions:

1. What is the staining material?
2. What is it on?
3. What is the safest treatment method that will remove the stain effectively without damaging the surface it's on?

Once you've thought over your approach, act promptly to apply a solution. If you're trying something new, test it on a hidden or inconspicuous place on whatever surface you're trying to clean. Try the mildest method first and move on to more severe treatments only if needed.

Tools and Treatments: A Stain-Removal Kit

NATURAL STAIN REMOVAL doesn't involve a lot of fancy equipment, but a few items are useful to have on hand in one place for a quick response when a stain occurs.

- A clean, light-colored, nonmetallic bucket (2 gallons [7.57 litres] is a good size) with a secure handle and a pouring spout. It's good for storing all other supplies, and may also be used for transporting water to stain-treatment sites or for soaking washable items.

❧ A clean, light-colored, nonmetallic laundry "tub" for soaking washable items, so they don't tie up your sink.

❧ A glass measuring cup (2- to 4-cup [470–940 ml] capacity) for measuring ingredients in stain-treatment solutions.

❧ A good supply of clean, white, or light-colored cloths, rags, old towels, or paper towels for blotting up spills; padding under stains that you're treating; blotting on stain treatments; and absorbing excess moisture when the stain is gone. Old (clean) athletic socks turned inside out make great applicators for blotting treatments onto stains, and when folded over, they work well as pads under small spots.

❧ A scraping tool. This may be an old, smooth-bladed, dull table knife; a plastic spoon; a spatula; or another item that lets you scrape and lift solid and semi-solid materials up and off of a surface.

❦ A set of measuring spoons for measuring ingredients in stain solutions. These should be dedicated for use in the laundry/cleaning cupboard to avoid contaminating food items with cleaning products.

❦ A small brush with a flat-bristle surface—not for scrubbing but for tamping (basically tapping with the bristles) stain treatments into a spot. An inexpensive toothbrush will work, as well.

❦ Spray bottles. One or two bottles to hold and apply stain-removal solutions. Label bottles with their contents. Rinse and wash them thoroughly if you switch to a different mixture. Use caution to avoid inadvertently mixing incompatible cleaning products.

In addition to keeping your tools handy, it's important to keep them clean. Rinse or wash everything you use after a stain-removal effort so it's ready to go the next time you need it.

The Stain-Fighters in Your Home

Although the list of materials you can use to treat a stain is fairly long, they generally fall into four categories: abrasives, absorbents, bleaching agents, and solvents. In treating a stain, you might use any or all of these types of stain-fighters, depending on the type of stain and the surface it's on.

Abrasives, such as baking soda and salt, are used to scrub and scour stains off of surfaces. They're most useful for stain removal on hard, mostly impervious surfaces.

Absorbents, which are powders or granules such as cornstarch or fuller's earth, are used to soak up liquid and oily stains from permeable surfaces—fabrics, unfinished wood, and carpet, for example.

Bleaching agents, including chlorine bleach and hydrogen peroxide, are used to remove colors from stains and may be a last resort when other methods fail to completely remove a spot. So-called oxygen, or "all-fabric" bleaches, may be added to the laundry to enhance the effects of pretreatments on washable fabrics.

Solvents, including water, household ammonia, vinegar, and isopropyl alcohol, work by diluting a staining agent and by keeping it in a solution so it can be flushed out of the fabric or surface it's on.

Handy Stain-Removal Solutions

Once you've assembled your stain-removal tools, take an inventory of stain-fighting materials. You may be surprised to discover how many you already have, and now's the time—before you're faced with a stain—to fill in any gaps in your supplies.

❧ **Alcohol** (isopropyl): a good solvent for some difficult stains, including grass and ink, but toxic and highly flammable; not a natural first choice, except in terms of efficacy; has antiseptic properties; requires sparing use in well-ventilated areas away from sparks, flames, or heat sources; necessitates the protection of skin and eyes and avoidance of prolonged exposure to its fumes; may cause some dyes to run; products labeled "rubbing alcohols," which may have fragrances and moisturizers added should not be used; must be diluted with water before being used on acetate, nylon, silk, and wool.

☙ **Ammonia** (ammonium hydroxide): on the alkaline side of the pH scale, ammonia is at the heart of many cleaning products; best to use clear ammonia without detergents added; good for breaking up grease stains and neutralizing acid stains; has a mild bleaching effect and is typically used in solution with water; should be used in a well-ventilated area and while eyes and skin are protected from contact; should be used on silk or wool; NEVER should be combined with chlorine bleach as dangerous, toxic fumes will result.

❦ **Baking soda** (sodium bicarbonate): the same ingredient you use to make your cookies rise also has applications as a stain-treatment; mildly alkaline with deodorizing abilities; works as a mild abrasive and as an absorbent for liquid or greasy stains; safe for almost any surface or fabric.

❦ **Bleach** (sodium hypochlorite, a.k.a. liquid chlorine bleach): just up the pH scale from ammonia is chlorine bleach, a powerful stain- and color-removing agent that's also found in many household cleaning products; a disinfectant that is effective for killing and cleaning up mildew; should be used only in diluted solutions and in well-ventilated areas; skin and eyes should be protected from contact; should not be used on wool, silk, leather, mohair, Spandex, noncolorfast fabrics, or on cottons or linens that have "wash-and-wear" finishes (such as wrinkle-resistance); NEVER should be combined with other cleaning products, especially ammonia, as dangerous, toxic fumes may result.

Why pH Matters

A quick chemistry lesson: Most cleansers are alkaline because most soiling agents are acidic. If you know whether a stain you're dealing with is acidic (most likely) or alkaline, you can neutralize it with an opposite product.

Neutralizing a stain loosens its hold on the surface and lessens its ability to cause damage such as bleaching. Bear in mind, however, that both acids and alkalis can set proteins, so be careful when dealing with combination stains (gravy, for example) that may have a protein component.

🍂 **Borax** (sodium tetraborate decahydrate): a mildly alkaline powder most often used as a laundry booster to enhance soil removal; a reasonably good deodorizer; useful in some stain-removal applications.

🍂 **Bran:** a safe, stable absorbent material for soaking up wet or oily stains on upholstery or carpets.

- **Club soda:** very slightly acidic, this popular drink mixer helps fizz away stains such as alcohol, coffee, tea, and red wine; safe and odorless; a good first treatment for old or mystery stains. Watch out for sweeteners and flavorings when shopping for club soda—you need the plain stuff for stain treatment.

- **Cornstarch:** silky textured powder used as a thickener in puddings, sauces, and soups; another handy absorbent that travels well from the kitchen to wherever it's needed to soak up wet or oily stains; a word of caution, however: its fine texture can make it difficult to get out of carpet and upholstery fibers.

- **Cream of tartar** (bitartrate of potassium): mildly acidic abrasive; used in cooking; sold with spices in the grocery store; may be mixed with water to make a paste for cleaning tarnish from metals or for lifting stains from colored fabrics.

Acid Stains

Most stains are acidic in nature, from hamburger fat to dirt, fruit juices, soft drinks, and tomatoes. As a general treatment, dilute acid stains by flushing them with water, neutralize with baking soda or ammonia solution, rinse with water, and blot or launder as usual. Washing soda or borax may be added to the washing machine to enhance the stain and soil removal.

❧ **Dishwashing liquid** (clear or white, near-neutral pH): made to clean dishes and cookware, it also is useful in treating stains from food and drinks; cuts greasy stains and loosens many others; in a mild solution with water, makes a fine laundry pretreatment. For stain-removal tasks, choose a product without added bleach, fragrance, or moisturizers.

🍃 **Erasers** (art gum and regular): mildly abrasive for rubbing away pencil marks, greasy spots, and dirty fingerprints on painted walls and wallpaper; keep a couple on hand for stain removal only, and rub them clean after use.

🍃 **Hair spray:** a solvent used to remove ink stains; success results from its high content of denatured alcohol, a highly toxic and flammable ingredient; conveniently comes in a handy spray bottle; should be used sparingly and in good ventilation; cheaper types tend to work better and have fewer additives that may contribute stains of their own; should be used with care if applying to acetate, silk, or wool.

🍃 **Hydrogen peroxide** (3-percent type used for first-aid, not for bleaching hair): a mild bleach; good for spot-treatment and "touching up" marks left after other stain-removal treatments have done a partial job; safe

Alkaline Stains

Alkaline stains include perspiration, grass, tarnish, mineral deposits, tannins (from tea and coffee), alcoholic drinks, and mustard. As a general treatment, flush with water to dilute the base, neutralize with a mild vinegar solution, rinse with water, and launder as usual. Other acids useful in treating alkaline stains include lemon juice and cream of tartar.

for most fabrics; loses its potency over time—buy only what you need, and discard any solution leftover after treating a stain.

◈ **Kitty litter** (nonclumping type): get the plainest kind available, and use as an absorbent for greasy or oily spills in your garage or driveway, or for large liquid cleanups like vomit.

☙ **Lemon juice** (citric acid): mild acid with gentle bleaching properties; traditionally used on alkaline stains such as coffee and tea or combined with salt to lift red wine spots; should be used with caution, if at all, on acid-sensitive fabrics (cotton, linen, rayon) and on acetate, silk, and wool.

☙ **Meat tenderizer** (unseasoned): a powdered enzyme product that may be mixed with water to make a paste for treating protein stains, especially blood; only unseasoned tenderizer should be used; should not be used on silk or wool.

☙ **Nail-polish remover** (nonacetone type, amyl acetate): strong solvent, although milder than acetone and safe for use on acetate fabric; a last resort for nail-polish spills; should be applied sparingly in a well-ventilated area away from sparks, flames, and heat sources; should avoid prolonged contact with fumes; requires protecting skin and eyes from contact.

❦ **Petroleum jelly** (white petrolatum): skin protectant; may be used to loosen greasy stains that have dried, to make them easier to remove from fabrics.

❦ **Salt** (sodium chloride): mildly abrasive; absorbent; may be combined with lemon juice or vinegar to clean tarnish; may be poured over coffee or red wine spills; forms a salt water solution for soaking stained washables.

❦ **Soap** (pure, as Ivory and Fels-Naptha): a mildly alkaline cleanser; useful for loosening oily or greasy stains; Should not be used on fruit stains, as it will set them.

❦ **Vegetable oil:** for loosening dried grease stains for easier removal; should be combined with abrasives (ashes, rottenstone) for rubbing the stains on finished wood.

- **Vinegar** (white distilled, a.k.a. acetic acid): inexpensive, mild acid used to neutralize alkaline residues from detergents; good for de-liming coffee pots and teapots; used in solution with water to treat stains; Should not be used on cotton, linen, or acetate.

- **WD-40**: petroleum-based penetrating lubricant spray; toxic and flammable; may be used to remove ink and dye stains and to soften adhesives and gum; not a natural first-choice; use in well-ventilated area and avoid prolonged exposure to fumes.

Household Help

You may also want to consider a few additions to the typical household stain-treatment supply:

- **Citrus solvents** (d-limonene): a natural alternative to harsh, petroleum-based solvents, and much safer for you and for the environment; still volatile; Should be used in well-ventilated areas in accordance with label directions. Stain removers with citrus solvents as the active ingredient are available in health food stores and from natural-product catalogs.

Boiling Water Treatment: Drivin

The boiling water treatment is more like an exorcism than a laundry procedure. You don't need any harsh chemicals to conduct this very dramatic and effective technique—just boiling water and a place where you can pour it safely. This method works well for removing fresh tea, coffee, wine, and fruit juice stains from cotton or linen fabrics.

To perform the boiling water treatment, stretch the fabric, stained-side down, over a heat-proof bowl or bucket, and secure it with a rubber band. Place the container and stained item some-place where any spatters will be contained—in a bathtub, for example. From a height of two to three feet (0.6-0.9 meters) above the fabric, pour boiling water through the stain.

❧ **Denatured alcohol** (ethyl alcohol, denatured by the addition of acetone or methanol): highly toxic and flammable; a powerful solvent sold in hardware stores; the main ingredient in making hair spray a successful stain remover; Should be used only as a

Out the Demons of Discoloration

Use care to avoid splashing yourself with boiling water and splattering the stain onto sur-rounding surfaces. If necessary, remove the fabric from the bucket, empty the now-dirty water, replace the fabric, and repeat the procedure. Don't pour the water in the bucket through the stretched fabric (unless you want to reapply the staining agent), and take care to avoid sloshing the dirty water onto the fabric when you remove it from the bucket.

Note that this treatment is the only exception to the rule about avoiding heat on sugar and protein stains, and it's only recommended for use on white or colorfast cottons or linens; the boiling water is too hot for most other fabric types.

last resort on nail polish, difficult grease stains, glues, and cements; Should be used in a well-ventilated area away from sparks, flames, and heat sources; avoid prolonged exposure to fumes; protect skin and eyes from contact; may cause dyes to run.

Look for Symbolism

The symbols on a garment's fabric-care label can teach you a good deal about how you should or should not treat stains. The triangles on the label may be of most interest, since they denote whether bleach may be used on a fabric. An open triangle indicates bleach tolerance; a "striped" triangle means only nonchlorine (all-fabric) bleach may be used; and a darkened triangle with an "X" over it means no bleach should be used.

To successfully treat stains without damaging suceptible fabrics, combine what you learn from the labels with the following tips on care for certain fabric types:

Acetate: susceptible to damage from vinegar, alcohol, and acetone; heat-sensitive

Acrylic: heat-sensitive

❧ **Enzyme cleaners:** products that actually digest protein stains; available from health food stores; may be applied as paste on stains or mixed with water for soaking stained items; should not be used on silk or wool.

Cotton: acids may damage cotton fibers; vinegar should not be applied

Linen: acids may damage linen fibers; vinegar should not be applied

Nylon: good stain resistance; slightly heat-sensitive

Polyester: resists some stains but prone to greasy stains; somewhat heat-sensitive

Ramie: acids may damage ramie fibers; vinegar should not be applied

Rayon: slightly acid sensitive; chlorine bleach may damage some types

Silk: do not use alcohol, ammonia, or strong alkalis, chlorine bleach, or enzymes; may require dry cleaning to avoid water spots

Spandex: do not use chlorine bleach—it takes the elasticity out of Spandex; heat-sensitive

Wool: do not use alcohol, ammonia, or strong alkalis, chlorine bleach, or enzymes

🌿 **Fuller's earth:** an absorbent once used to clean wool, fuller's earth may be found in hobby stores and home centers; its darker color makes it useful for soaking up liquid and greasy stains on dark fabrics.

🌿 **Glycerin:** a vegetable oil by-product of soap-making, sold in health food stores; highly water-absorbent; good for loosening soil in stains and also in rehydrating dried stains to make them easier to remove.

🌿 **Rottenstone** (a.k.a. Tripoli): a fine, powdered pumice used in wood finishing and for polishing musical instruments and wood gun stocks; available from woodworking suppliers; may be mixed with linseed oil to use as a mild abrasive to remove stains and water marks from finished wood.

🌿 **Washing soda** (sodium carbonate): a slightly caustic, alkaline, mined mineral used as a laundry booster; may be substituted for solvents in treating greasy stains; good odor neutralizer; Should not be used on wool or silk fabrics; Should not be used on aluminum surfaces, no-wax floors, or fiberglass sinks, tubs, or tile.

Protein Stains

(Animal-Related; Blood, Eggs, Bodily Fluids, Etc.)

I
T'S PRETTY EASY TO KNOW when you're dealing with a protein stain: If the stain has an animal origin, it is protein in nature. Dairy products, infant formulas, eggs, gelatin, and meat juices all are sources of protein stains, as are the full array of bodily fluids, both human and animal. This latter group of protein stains has a high "ick" factor, but treating protein stains doesn't have to be difficult if you keep your cool.

Cool water is the first treatment for protein stains. For most washable fabrics, you can flush a protein-based stain away with plenty of cool water; if a spot remains, soak the item in cold water. Heating proteins changes their chemical structure (think about browning meat or how an egg white changes on a hot surface or in hot water). Exposing proteins to acids can have a similar effect (think about how milk curdles when it comes in contact with vinegar or lemon juice). When these types of changes take place, protein stains become much harder to eliminate. Exceptions to this rule include hardened glue, for which you'll need to heat in order to remove, and feces stains, which are treated with warm water.

Although treatments for specific protein stains vary, you'll be more successful in removing all of them if you remember to stick with neutral (pH 7) to mildly alkaline stain-removal solutions. You also can treat protein stains with enzyme solutions, which digest proteins. Enzyme-based cleaners are available from health-food stores and natural cleaning supply companies; unseasoned meat tenderizer may be used to treat protein stains, too—when you tenderize meat, you're using enzymes to pre-digest it.

In this chapter, you'll find solutions for the following protein stains:

Baby formula	Meat juice
Bird droppings	Milk
Blood	Perspiration
Eggs	Pet stains
Feces	Ring around the collar
Fly specks	Urine
Glue (washable and	Yogurt
school paste)	Vomit (and mucus)
Ice cream	

BABY FORMULA

On white clothing/washable fabric:

❧ Treat the stain with undiluted lemon juice and put the item in the sun.

On colored clothing/washable fabric:

❧ Coat the stain with a paste made of cool water and unseasoned meat tenderizer; let set for at least 30 minutes, then brush away the paste and launder as usual.

❧ Soak in an enzyme solution according to the item's label directions.

❧ In a pinch, wipe up formula spills and spit-ups with moist baby wipes. Rinse with cool water, and treat any remaining stain as soon as possible.

BIRD DROPPINGS
On clothing/washable fabric:

❧ Gently scrape away any residue, taking care to avoid pushing the stain further into the fabric. Flush with cool water until the stain is gone. Use hydrogen peroxide or a bleach safe for the fabric on any remaining stain (test a hidden area for colorfastness) before laundering as usual.

On canvas (such as awnings or patio furniture cushions):

❦ Dampen a scrub brush, and rub the bristles over a bar of Fels-Naptha soap, then sprinkle them with dry washing soda. Scrub away the bird droppings with your soapy brush, then rinse thoroughly with clear water. Beware of the "clean spot syndrome" that may result from this treatment—you may find yourself scrubbing the entire awning to get it as clean as the place the birds besmirched!

BLOOD

On clothing/washable fabric:

❦ Treat blood stains promptly with cool water, and keep them moist until they've been completely removed—once dried, blood is much harder to get out. Because heat will set blood stains in fabrics, avoid ironing or hot-air drying until the stain is entirely gone.

Beyond Babies' Bottoms: Baby Wipes vs. Blood

Busy mom Erana B. of Bethlehem, Pennsylvania, reports that baby wipes have saved her garments from many stains. "One day when my daughter was learning to walk, she fell while 'cruising' the furniture and bumped her mouth on the edge of a table. I picked her up to comfort her and, in the process of calming her crying, wound up with blood from a cut on her lip all over my shirt. I cleaned it off with wipes because they were handy, and they removed the stain completely," she says. Erana adds that wipes meant for baby bottoms work well for removing a variety of other stains, too, including food spills and ballpoint ink.

❧ Rinse with copious amounts of cold water, then soak in cold salt water (1 cup [240 g] of salt in 2 quarts [1.9 L] of water). Rub mild soap (such as Ivory) on any remaining stain, and rinse with cold water; launder as usual once stain is lifted.

On white fabric only:

❧ Treat the stain with hydrogen peroxide.

On upholstery:

❧ Make a paste of cornstarch and cool water, and rub it lightly into the stain, covering it completely. If possible, place the stained item in the sun to dry. Brush away the dried paste and repeat as needed. Or, coat the stain with a paste made from unseasoned meat tenderizer and cool water. Let set for 15 to 30 minutes, then brush away, and sponge with cool water.

On a mattress:

❧ Treat light stains with a thick paste of baking soda and water; brush away when the paste has dried. Treat a heavily stained mattress by propping it on its side (this keeps both the stain and the treatment from soaking further into the mattress). Press an old towel or other thick cloth into the mattress below the stain, then sponge the area with cold salt water (¼ cup [55 g] of salt in 2 cups [475 ml] of water). Once the stain is lifted, rinse with cold water, and blot with clean cloths or paper towels. Let the mattress dry before laying it flat.

On carpet:

🌿 Sponge with club soda or cold water until stain is lifted. Or, sprinkle salt over the stain, then flush with cold water; blot thoroughly. You can also apply a paste of unseasoned meat tenderizer and cold water, then sponge it off with cool water after 30 minutes.

EGG

On clothing/washable fabric:

🌿 Soak in 2 quarts (1.9 L) of cold water with 2 tablespoons (28 g) of salt added. Sponge the stain with the cold salt water. Combine ¼ teaspoon (1.25 ml) of dishwashing liquid in ½ cup (120 ml) of lukewarm water with a few drops of ammonia, and blot onto the stain. Rinse with clear cool water, and launder as usual. If the stain is still evident, make a paste of unseasoned meat tenderizer and water, and apply to the spot; leave in place for 30 minutes, then shake off the paste and rinse with cold water. Launder again.

Remove Small Bloodstains Lickety-*Spit*

A drop of blood, which could result from a slip of a needle, for example, needn't spell doom for needlework, says quilt book author Sue B. of New Tripoli, Pennsylvania. Most experienced seamstresses know this secret, says Sue: To remove a small spot of blood from your sewing, all you need is a bit of your own saliva. Quicker than you can say, "Pass the Band-Aids," the spit will dissolve the bloodstain, so you can resume stitching (with a bit more caution).

On carpet/upholstery:

❧ Use a spoon or dull knife to lift up any egg on the surface. Blot with ample amounts of cold salt water, followed by clear water, then blot dry with white cloths or paper towels. If a spot remains, sponge with 1 cup (235 ml) of cool water with ½ teaspoon (2.5 ml) of dishwashing liquid, rinse, and blot dry.

Over-Easy–Not So Easy

We all know what happens to an egg when it's heated–and the result is certainly not something we'd like to see on our clothes or carpet. Avoid using hot water to clean up egg stains, and don't hot-air dry fabrics until you're sure all the egg has been removed. If you "cook" the egg on your garment or carpeting, you'll set the stain very securely.

FECES (*SEE ALSO* PET STAINS, PAGE 76)
On carpet/upholstery:

- Carefully clean up all solid material to avoid spreading the stain. Add a few drops of ammonia to warm water, and sponge any remaining spots. Rinse with clear, warm water, and blot thoroughly with clean cloths.

- In a pinch, use baby wipes to tidy up—this is what they're made for, after all.

FLY SPECKS
On windows:

- Wipe with a soft cloth dampened with denatured alcohol, rubbing firmly to remove the deposits.

GLUE
On clothing/washable fabric:

- Use a damp cloth or sponge to wipe up glue drips and spills while they're still wet. Water-based glues become water resistant—and thus harder to remove—as they dry. After wiping up wet glue, launder as usual.

꙰ For dried, gel-type washable glue, pre-soak for 10 minutes in cold water, then launder as usual.

꙰ For dried, white, washable glue, soak in the hottest water that's safe for the fabric. Once the glue has softened, gently scrape off as much as possible. Launder as usual in the hottest water recommended for the fabric.

On carpet:

꙰ Thoroughly wet a clean rag with warm water, and lay it on top of the glue spot. Leave it for about an hour to soften the glue, then rub the glue spot with a wet cloth, using a circular motion. Repeat until you've removed all of the glue, and blot with dry cloths.

‌ὥ Soak the glue spot with undiluted white vinegar, then use a dull knife or spoon to scrape it up and out of the carpet fibers. Rinse the spot with warm water, then blot dry. Persistent spots (and rubber-based glues) may require treatment with natural-solvent spot removers.

‌ὥ As a last resort, use nail scissors or other delicate cutters to snip dried glue out of the carpet pile.

ICE CREAM

On clothing/washable fabric:

‌ὥ Remove as much solid and liquid material as possible, then rinse with cool water. Add 1 teaspoon (5 ml) of dishwashing liquid to a cup (235 ml) of lukewarm water, and sponge on the stain, then launder as usual. If the flavoring in the ice cream has left a stain that remains after laundering, treat it according to the type of stain it is (e.g., chocolate, fruit, etc.) Heat sets sugar stains, so don't use hot water or hot-air drying until you're sure the stain is out.

MEAT JUICE (*SEE* BLOOD, PAGE 65)

MILK

On clothing/washable fabric:

🍃 Soak up spills immediately, and sponge or rinse with cool water. Apply a solution of ¼ teaspoon (1.25 ml) of clear dishwashing liquid in ½ cup (120 ml) of luke-warm water to spots before laundering in cool water. Don't put the garment in the dryer until you're certain the stain is gone. If a spot remains after washing, soak it in an enzyme solution according to the label directions, or apply a paste made of unseasoned meat tenderizer and cool water, letting it set for 30 minutes. Brush off the paste, and wash the item again in cool water. (Do not use enzyme cleaners on silk or wool.)

On upholstery:

🍃 Blot up the spill, and sponge with lukewarm water until all milk residue is gone. Blot dry with clean cloths or white paper towels.

PERSPIRATION

On clothing/washable fabric:

❧ Sponge stained areas with a solution made by dissolving 4 tablespoons (60 g) of salt in 1 quart (946 ml) of hot water, or soak in warm water with 3–4 tablespoons (45–60 g) of salt dissolved in it.

❧ Rub fresh stains with bar soap, such as Ivory or Fels-Naptha, before laundering.

❧ Soak stained clothing overnight in 3 gallons (11.3 L) of water with ¼ cup (60 ml) of white vinegar. (Don't soak cotton, linen, silk, or acetate in vinegar—it can damage these fabrics.)

❧ You also can make a solution of 1 teaspoon (5 ml) of household ammonia in 2 cups (946 ml) of cold water, and sponge it on fresh stains. (Don't use ammonia on silk or wool.) Rinse well with cold water. Launder as usual after any of these treatments.

❦ Coat stained areas with a paste of baking soda and water; let set for 30 minutes before brushing it off, then launder as usual.

❦ For perspiration stains on silk or wool, add ¾ teaspoon (3.8 ml) of rosemary essential oil to ½ cup (120 ml) of hydrogen peroxide, and pour into a spray bottle. Shake well to mix ingredients and while using it on the stain. Test colorfastness on an inconspicuous part of the garment before using the mixture. Spray to saturate stains; then let set for ½ hour.

❦ Launder as usual after any of these treatments. Heat from hot-air drying or ironing can set perspiration stains. Make sure the stains are gone before applying heat to your garments.

PET STAINS

Urine, on carpet/upholstery:

❦ Blot up as much of the liquid as you can, as quickly

as possible, using white cloths or white paper towels. Sponge the area with ¼ teaspoon (1.25 ml) of clear dishwashing liquid in 1 cup (235 ml) of warm water, then blot with a clean cloth, and repeat until the visible stain is gone. Be sure to blot up the solution in between applications to avoid overwetting your carpet or upholstery and flushing the urine into the padding.

Next, use a clean cloth to apply a solution of 1 part white vinegar in 2 parts water, sponging it on, and then blotting with dry cloths or paper towels. Cover the treated area with fresh, dry toweling, and weight it down to increase moisture absorption. Change the toweling repeatedly until no more moisture is being absorbed.

❧ Pet stores carry enzyme-based cleaning products designed specifically to remove the stain and smell associated with urine accidents. If you're training a puppy or dealing with a territorial cat, consider one of these spot-specific products for ease of (repeated) use.

Don't Risk Repeats– Avoid Ammonia

Bypass the ammonia when you're looking through your cleaning supplies for something to remove pet urine spots. The scent of ammonia may make your pet more likely to return to the scene of the crime for a repeat performance.

Pet vomit, on carpet:

❧ Cover pet vomit with a thick layer of baking soda, and wait until the baking soda soaks up the moisture from the mess. Once it's dried, lift or vacuum up the residue. Follow with club soda if any stain remains, then blot thoroughly with clean cloths or paper towels.

"RING AROUND THE COLLAR"

On shirt collars and cuffs:

❧ Make a solution of 2 tablespoons (30 ml) ammonia, 1 teaspoon (5 ml) clear dishwashing liquid, and 2 cups (475 ml) warm water, and pour into a spray bottle. Use as a laundry pretreatment, spraying on stains and leaving the garment for 15 minutes before laundering as usual.

❧ Make a paste of vinegar and baking soda (don't worry, it will stop fizzing after a few seconds), and rub it into stains before laundering.

❧ Shampoo is sometimes recommended for removing a "ring around the collar," since it is designed to wash away the same dirt and oils from hair and skin that cause stains on the inside of shirt collars. But shampoo often contains moisturizers, fragrances, and other ingredients that are nicer for your hair than they are for your shirt collar. Use it in a pinch—brush it onto

Cure a Common Cat Woe with Club Soda

Cats get hairballs. And cats that have hairballs are bound to cough them up someplace—usually in the middle of a carpet, or on your favorite upholstered chair. After years of trying various (stinky, toxic) chemical cleaners with mostly inadequate results, I turned to club soda. Now it's all I use when my cat Roxy leaves a "present" on the rug. I just scoop up as much of the solid material as possible, then pour on the club soda. After a couple of minutes, I blot the area dry with a clean cloth.

collar stains before laundering—but choose the clearest, plainest brand you have available to avoid replacing one stain with another.

URINE (*SEE ALSO* PET STAINS, PAGE 76)

On clothing/washable fabric:

☙ Rinse as quickly as possible with cool water, then soak in warm water for 30 minutes. Wash in warm water, adding ½ cup (115 g) of borax to the load. If a spot remains after laundering, soak in an enzyme solution (not for silk or wool), or blot with hydrogen peroxide (on light fabrics only; test for colorfastness before using). Wash again.

On carpet:

☙ Act quickly to blot up as much liquid as possible, then flush or sponge the spot with cool water or club soda, blotting and reapplying until no stain remains. Sponge with ¼ teaspoon (1.25 ml) clear dishwashing liquid in 1 cup (235 ml) warm water, blot, rinse with clear water, and blot dry with clean cloths or white paper towels.

There's the Smell, As Well

"My husband doesn't stink!" exclaimed my friend Mona, when she saw me at the weekly farmer's market. "He got sprayed by a skunk this morning," she added, explaining that she'd used a safe and simple solution to rid her spouse of the pungent smell of a "direct hit" from a skunk. Mona's mixture was 1 cup (235 ml) of 3 percent hydrogen peroxide with 1 tablespoon (15 g) of baking soda and a "squirt" of dishwashing liquid stirred in. She put the solution in a spray bottle and let her husband have it—with remarkable results: The man did not smell of skunk.

Since the smell from a urine accident can be as bad, or worse than, the visible stain, it's useful to know that this same solution will take the stink out of errant puppy piddles and cat territorial markers. The mild hydrogen peroxide in this solution will not fade fabrics, so it's safe for use on most surfaces, including fabrics and carpeting. (If you're concerned, test on a hidden spot first.) Spray it on, wait for a few minutes, then sponge or rinse with clear water.

YOGURT

On clothing/washable fabric:

❦ Use a spoon to scoop up any yogurt on the surface of the fabric; blot up any liquid with a clean cloth or paper towel. Thoroughly rinse or sponge the spot with cool water, then blot on a solution of ¼ teaspoon (1.25 ml) clear dishwashing liquid in ½ cup (120 ml) lukewarm water. Wash in cool water and air dry. Treat persistent stains by soaking them in an enzyme solution (do not use on silk or wool); wash again.

VOMIT

On clothing/washable fabric:

❦ Quickly clean up any solid material, and flush the soiled area with cool water. Add 1 teaspoon (5 ml) of clear dishwashing liquid and 2 tablespoons (28 ml) of ammonia to 1 quart (946 ml) of warm water, and soak the item in it for at least 30 minutes, agitating occasionally to help loosen the stain. Rinse with cool

water; if the stain is gone, wash in warm water with
½ cup (115 g) of borax added. If a stain persists,
soak it in an enzyme solution (not for silk or wool)
according to label directions, and wash again in
warm water.

On carpet/upholstery:

❦ Scrape up solid material, and blot up liquid, removing
as much of the stain as possible. Act quickly to rinse
or sponge the spot with cool water to prevent damage from the acids in the vomit. Blot with clean
cloths or paper towels, and sponge with more water.
Blot again, then add 1 teaspoon (5 g) of borax to 2
cups (475 ml) of warm water, and sponge over the
spot. Blot and rinse with clear water; use dry cloths
or paper towels to remove as much of the water
from the carpet or cushions as possible.

Tannin Stains

(Plant-Related: Coffee, Tea, Fruit, Wine, Etc.)

JUST AS PROTEIN STAINS come from animal sources, tannin stains have plant origins. The word "tannin" comes from the centuries-old practice of tanning leather by using plant compounds to preserve and waterproof it. Tannins represent many of the first dyes and paints used by humans. Indeed, many of the tannin stains in this book, including beets, coffee, tea, and red wine, are known for their ability to leave permanent stains.

The good news is that tannin stains are water-soluble and often can be flushed out of fabrics with ample amounts of clear, cool water, or cool water with a small amount of vinegar added. But remember how heat changes the chemistry of proteins? It also sets sugar, which often accompanies tannin stains. The only heat-related recourse recommended for tannin stains is the boiling water method, for use on fabrics that can tolerate such harsh treatment (*see* "Boiling Water Treatment: Driving Out the Demons of Discoloration," page 54).

Tannin stains can be very persistent, and the older they get, the harder they are to remove. Prompt treatment is essential to avoid difficult stains that only bleaching agents will remove. There's a reason why our ancestors used many of these materials to color their paints and dye their fabrics.

In this chapter, you will find solutions for the following tannin stains:

Alcoholic beverages
Barbecue sauce
Beer
Beets
Berries
Chocolate
Coffee
Cola
Curry
Fruit/fruit juice
Grass
Ink (ballpoint, watercolor, washable)
Jams and jellies
Ketchup
Maple syrup
Marker (washable)
Mustard
Perfume and cologne
Pollen
Red wine
Soft drinks
Soy sauce
Spaghetti sauce
Syrup
Tea
Tomato
Wine

ALCOHOLIC BEVERAGES

On clothing/washable fabric:

✷ Soak stained area with club soda; blot thoroughly.

ǁ Soak in cold water mixed with 1–3 tablespoons (15–45 ml) of glycerin; rinse with equal parts white vinegar and water.

ǁ After either of the preceding treatments, launder as usual.

On carpet/upholstery:

ǁ Sponge with club soda until the stain disappears.

ǁ Sponge with 1 quart (946 ml) of warm water to which you've added 1 teaspoon (5 ml) of dishwashing liquid. Blot, then sponge-rinse with clear, warm water; blot and repeat until all solution is removed.

ǁ Sponge with a solution made with equal parts glycerin and water.

❧ Treat persistent stains with 2 tablespoons (28 ml) of ammonia in 1 cup (235 ml) water. Rinse well, then apply 1 cup (235 ml) of white vinegar mixed with 2 cups (470 ml) of water; blot and rinse with clear, warm water.

Beware the Bathroom Blow-Dryer

Getting doused by a drink while dining out can make the hot-air dryer in the restaurant restroom seem like a good option for drying up the damp spots on your clothing. But alcohol, and mixers such as fruit juice and soda, contain sugar, and heat will set a sugar stain, creating a yellow-brown spot that's really tough to remove. To avoid this, flush that stain with generous amounts of club soda and/or lukewarm water, blotting with cloth napkins or paper towels as you go. If you can't resist the urge to push the button on the blower, do everything you can to rinse away the original spill before stepping up to the dryer. Stay away from the soap dispenser, too, if your drink was one of those fruity beverages—soap can set a fruit stain in fabric.

After any wet treatments on carpeting or upholstery, blot thoroughly and repeatedly with clean, dry cloths; set a fan to blow over the area to promote complete drying.

On finished wood:

Clean up spills promptly; treat spots with oil-based cleaner/polish.

Rub old stains with a paste made of rottenstone or powdered pumice, and linseed oil. Apply lightly with the grain, then wipe with a soft cloth moistened with linseed oil; polish.

BARBECUE SAUCE (*SEE* KETCHUP, PAGE 117)

BEER
On clothing/washable fabric:

Rinse the stained area with cool water, then sponge with a solution of 2 tablespoons (28 ml) of white vinegar, 2 cups (475 ml) of water, and 1 teaspoon (5 ml) of dishwashing liquid. Launder as usual.

On upholstery:

❧ Soak up the spill, then sponge the area with cool water; blot thoroughly once the stain is lifted. Sponge dried stains with equal parts water and white vinegar, blot thoroughly, and rinse with clear, warm water. Blot well with clean cloths to dry.

On carpet:

❧ Soak up the spill, then sponge the area with club soda or warm water until the stain is gone. If the spot persists, sponge on a solution of 1 tablespoon (15 ml) of ammonia in ½ cup (120 ml) of water; blot the solution and then rinse with clear water. Use 1 part vinegar to 2 parts water to neutralize the ammonia, then blot and rinse again.

@ Alcohol may lift old stains (test on a hidden or inconspicuous spot first). Dampen a cloth with iso-propyl alcohol, and blot it on the stain, working from the outer edges inward. Change the cloth often, and blot with a clean, dry cloth when done.

@ Finish by blotting thoroughly and using a fan or dehumidifier, if necessary, to dry the treated area.

BEETS

On white, washable cotton or linen:

@ Rinse with cold, running water. If the fabric will tolerate it, stretch the item "face down" over a bucket or sink, and coat the stain with laundry borax. Carefully pour very hot to boiling water from a height of 2 feet (0.6 m) over the stain. Repeat as necessary; launder as usual once the stain is gone.

On white or colored clothing/washable fabric:

@ Rinse with cold, running water, then soak in solution

of 1 tablespoon (15 g) of laundry borax in 2 cups (475 ml) of warm water. Launder as usual once the stain is lifted.

BERRIES

On all washable fabrics:

🌿 Act quickly. Red and purple berry stains don't take long to become permanent. Rinse or flush the stain with cold running water until no more color is coming out of the stain.

On sturdy, white, or colorfast clothing and washable fabric:

🌿 On fresh stains only, try the boiling water method on durable cottons and linens. Stretch the fabric stain-side down over a heat-proof bowl or bucket. Place the bucket in a bathtub or someplace where splashing is not a concern, and carefully pour boiling water through the stain from a height of 2 to 3 feet (0.6–0.9 m). Use caution to avoid splashing yourself with boiling water and to keep from splattering the surrounding area with hot water and berry juice. Empty the water in the container and repeat as necessary. Once the stain is gone, launder as usual.

On other clothing and washable fabric:

❧ After flushing with cold water until no more color is released, soak the stain in undiluted lemon juice, or rub a freshly cut lemon over the stain, and let set for 30 minutes. Rinse with cool water, launder as usual, and air dry.

❧ Loosen dried stains by soaking for an hour in a solution of equal parts glycerin and lukewarm water. Then flush with cool water, blot, and apply lemon juice as above.

❧ Use a soft cloth dipped in denatured alcohol to dab persistent stains. Place a clean, absorbent cloth pad under the stain, and refold it as color transfers from

Apples and Oranges vs. Berries and Cherries

When my sons were small, I came to the conclusion that apple juice was preferable to red fruit punch, and white grape juice was better than purple grape juice. I based these choices solely on the color of the juices in question—no need to worry about swabbing up dark red spills on the couch or deep purple spots from the rug. What I didn't consider was how insidious those light-colored fruit juices could be in creating stains of their own.

Because they go on almost clearly, light-colored juices such as apple, pear, citrus, and white grape are easy to blot and forget—until they've been washed (without any dilution or pretreatment) and dried (without the juice being sufficiently removed). Unfortunately, the sugary residue from those near-clear juices hangs around without a brilliant red stain to remind you to pretreat before washing and drying. The result: freshly laundered clothing with unexpected (and almost impossible to remove) yellow-brown stains set by the heat of the dryer and the passage of time. Live and learn: I still prefer to arm my sons and youthful visitors with light-colored juices, but I now know to treat all juice spills with equal care.

the stain onto the padding. Launder as usual once the stain is gone; air dry.

On carpet/upholstery:

✹ Soak up as much liquid as possible. Sponge the stain with cold water, and blot with clean cloths, repeating until the stain is lifted. Blot thoroughly with clean, dry cloths.

✹ Dab persistent stains with a cloth dampened with isopropyl alcohol (test colorfastness on a hidden place first), changing the cloth as color transfers from the stain. Sponge with cool water or club soda, and blot thoroughly.

CHOCOLATE

On clothing/washable fabric:

✹ Gently scrape away any chocolate on the surface, then blot the stain with cold water. If the spot remains, add 1 teaspoon (5 ml) of clear dishwashing liquid to 1 cup (235 ml) of cool water, and sponge onto the stain with a clean cloth. Rinse thoroughly with cool water. If the stain persists, your next step depends upon the type of chocolate:

- If it's *milk chocolate*, add a few drops of ammonia to your dishwashing liquid solution, and blot and rinse the spot again. A stain that persists after these treatments may require laundering with a bleach safe for the fabric.

- If it's *dark chocolate*, add 2 tablespoons (28 ml) of white vinegar to the dishwashing liquid solution, blot, and rinse the spot again. If there's still a stain, use a clean cloth to blot it with hydrogen peroxide.

- For difficult stains on fabric that can tolerate hot water, stretch the stain over a heat-proof bowl or bucket, and sprinkle borax over the stain. Pour hot-to-boiling water through the stain, taking care to avoid splashing yourself.

On carpet:

🌿 Gently scrape up any chocolate on the surface of the carpet, blot up any liquid spills, and sponge the stain with cold water. Blot dry with clean cloths or paper towels, then blot glycerin onto the spot. Blot and rinse with cool water.

COFFEE

On the bottom of a carafe/coffee pot:

🌿 Quarter a lemon, and mix its juice with 2 tablespoons (28 g) of salt in the bottom of the coffee pot. Add ice to cover the bottom, swish it around until the stains are gone, then empty and wash it as usual.

On coffee cups:

🌿 Sprinkle salt on your sponge, and wipe the stained area. Or wet the stains with white vinegar, and wipe with a damp sponge sprinkled with baking soda or salt. Let it soak until stains are lifted.

🌿 Fill cups or carafe with water, and toss in a denture-cleaning tablet. Let soak for 3 to 4 hours before washing as usual.

On clothing/washable fabric:

🌿 For coffee with cream, rinse first with cold water, then hot, before laundering as usual.

🌿 Cover wet stains with baking soda to absorb excess moisture. Brush or shake off the baking soda, and sponge the stain with 1 cup (235 ml) of vinegar, 1 tablespoon (15 ml) of dishwashing liquid and ½ cup (120 ml) of water. Let set for 15 minutes; launder as usual.

🌿 Place the item over a bucket or sink, and carefully pour boiling water through the stained area.

On nonwashable fabric:

❧ Treat the stain with a solution made of equal parts isopropyl alcohol and glycerin, then blot with clean cloths or paper towels. Repeat treatment as necessary, then clean the item according to label instructions.

On upholstery:

❧ Mix 1 tablespoon (15 g) of borax in 2 cups (473 ml) of water, and sponge over the stained area, or combine equal parts warm water and glycerin, and apply to stain. After either treatment, blot thoroughly with clean, dry cloths or paper towels.

❧ If you have a bottle of Wine Away (www.wineaway.com) in your cleaning cupboard, spray it on the spot, and follow label instructions for stain removal. In addition to wine stains, this water-based product works well on other tannin stains, including coffee and tea. (*See* "A Speedy Solution for Wine Spills," page 126)

On carpet:

🍃 Soak up excess liquid, then sponge the stain with ample amounts of club soda or cold water. If the stain persists, try a solution of 1 teaspoon (5 g) of borax in 1 cup (235 ml) of water, or treat difficult spots with hydrogen peroxide, blotting after 15 minutes. Finish by rinsing with cold water or club soda, then blot thoroughly with clean, dry cloths or paper towels.

🍃 Soak up the spill, then treat it with a solution of 1 tablespoon (15 ml) of white vinegar in 1 cup (235 ml) of water with a few drops of dishwashing liquid added. Follow with club soda or clear water, and blot dry.

On marble hearth or countertop:

🍃 Pour salt over the stain to prevent it from soaking in. As the salt absorbs the coffee, brush it away and apply fresh salt, repeating until the stain is gone. If it persists, pour milk over a new application of salt, and let it set for a few hours before wiping with a damp cloth.

COLA

On clothing/washable fabric:

🍃 Blot up the spill with white paper towels, then sprinkle on baking soda to absorb more of the liquid. Brush or shake off the baking soda, then sponge the stain with cool, clear water, and blot with paper towels or clean cloths. If a spot is still apparent, mix a solution of 2 parts white vinegar to 1 part water with 1-2 teaspoons (5-10 ml) of clear dishwashing liquid and ¼-½ teaspoon (1.25-2.5 ml) of rosemary essential oil, and dab it onto the stain with a clean cloth. Leave this on the fabric for 15 minutes before laundering as usual. If the stain remains after laundering, wash again with a bleach safe for the fabric. Make sure the spot is gone before you dry the garment; hot-air drying will set a sugary soda stain.

On carpet/upholstery:

☙ Blot up the spill with white paper towels, then sprinkle on baking soda to absorb more of the liquid. Brush, shake, or vacuum away the baking soda, then sponge the stain with tepid water to which you've added ¼ teaspoon (1.25 ml) of clear dishwashing liquid, blotting and rinsing repeatedly until the stain is removed. Finish by blotting thoroughly with clean, dry cloths or paper towels.

CURRY

On clothing/washable fabric:

☙ Rinse the stain with lukewarm water; mix ¼ cup (60 ml) of glycerin with ¼ cup (60 ml) of warm water, and work into the spot. Let set for 30 minutes, then rinse with lukewarm water. Launder as usual, using borax along with your normal detergent. If the stain persists after laundering, treat it with hydrogen peroxide.

On carpet:

❧ Wipe or scrape up as much of the stain as possible, then rub glycerin into the spot to loosen the stain. Mix 1 tablespoon (28 g) of borax in 2 cups (475 ml) of warm water, and blot it onto the stain; rinse with clear, warm water, and blot dry. Repeat as necessary until the stain is gone.

FRUIT/FRUIT JUICE
On clothing/washable fabric:

❧ Blot up the spill with white paper towels, then sprinkle on baking soda to absorb more of the liquid. Brush or shake off the baking soda, then sponge the stain with cool, clear water (or rinse the entire garment), and blot with paper towels or clean cloths. If a spot is still apparent, mix a solution of 2 parts white vinegar to 1 part water with 1–2 teaspoons (5–10 ml) of clear dishwashing liquid and ¼–½ teaspoon (1.25–2.5 ml) of rosemary essential oil, and dab it onto the stain with a clean cloth. Leave this on the fabric for 15 minutes before laundering as usual. If the stain remains after laundering, wash again with a bleach that is safe for the fabric. Make sure the spot is gone before you dry the garment; hot-air drying will set a sugary stain.

❦ Apply fresh lemon juice to the stain, and leave it for 30 minutes, then launder in cool water, using a bleach appropriate for the fabric.

❦ For deep-colored stains on sturdy white or colorfast fabrics, sponge with cool water until no more color transfers from the spot. Stretch the stained fabric over a heat-proof bowl or bucket, with the stain facing downward, and secure it with a rubber band. Set the bucket in your bathtub or another place where splashing will be contained. Carefully pour boiling water through the stain from 2 to 3 feet (0.6–0.9 meters) above it. If the spot persists (and for fabrics that can't tolerate the boiling water treatment), apply fresh lemon juice to the stain, then rinse with water, blot thoroughly, and let air dry.

🍃 Treat dark fruit stains with Wine Away stain remover. This commercially available product is made of safe, natural ingredients and works remarkably well on many difficult stains, including red wine and deep-colored fruit juices. Check www.wineaway.com to find local retail sources or to order from the manufacturer.

On carpet/upholstery:

🍃 Blot the spill, then sponge it with club soda or cool water, blot with clean cloths, and repeat until no more color transfers from the stain. Add ¼ teaspoon (1.25 ml) of dishwashing liquid to ½ cup (120 ml) of cool water, and sponge on the stain; rinse with clear water, and blot dry. If a spot remains, treat with Wine Away or Red Erase (www.wineaway.com and www.rederase.com), following label directions.

Keep Your Cool with Fruit Stains

With their bright colors and sugary constitutions, fruit stains can seem daunting from the moment they hit their target. Quick action and cool temperatures are the keys to making these spots do a quick fade. Avoid using heat, alkaline cleaners, or soaps; all of these will set fruit stains. Keep stained fabrics out of the dryer and away from your iron until you're sure the stain is fully removed.

GRASS STAINS

On clothing/washable fabric:

🌿 Put a pad of clean cloths or white paper towels under the stain. Sponge with undiluted white vinegar. If the stain persists, make a paste of cream of tartar and water, and apply it to the spot. Let it dry, then brush off the paste, and launder as usual.

Get Sour on Grass

Alkaline cleansers such as ammonia, baking soda, borax, and washing soda can set grass stains. Stick with acidic treatments, such as vinegar and cream of tartar. Alcohol is a solvent that works well for getting out the grass, but it may cause dyes in clothing to run (test colorfastness on a hidden or inconspicuous place before applying).

Sponge the stain with lukewarm water, then moisten a cloth with isopropyl alcohol, and blot it over the stain until it is gone. (Test on a hidden part of the garment before applying alcohol; dilute 1 part alcohol to 2 parts water for acetate fabrics and noncolorfast materials.) Launder as usual.

❧ If the stain persists, treat with a paste of unseasoned meat tenderizer and water. Let dry, then brush away paste.

❧ Soak in enzyme solution, according to label directions. Launder with bleach that is safe for the fabric.

INK (BALLPOINT)
On clothing/washable fabric:

❧ Put potential solutions to the test: If you know which of your dozens of pens the ink stain came from, mark a scrap of fabric similar to the item you need to treat, and try different removal methods to see which works best on that ink and fabric.

❧ Place a cloth or paper towel under the stained item, and sponge the stain with lukewarm water until no more ink transfers out of the stain. Next, soak the mark with hair spray, and blot until no more color leaves the stain. Sponge with warm water and a squirt of dishwashing liquid, then launder. Proceed with stronger solvents (isopropyl alcohol, denatured alcohol, nail polish remover) as needed if the stain lingers after laundering. Alcohol (including the alcohol in hair spray) can cause dyes in fabrics to run; test on a hem or seam allowance before applying on a visible part of the item.

❧ Soak the stain in milk for 1 hour, then coat it with a paste of vinegar and cornstarch. Brush away the dried paste, and launder as usual. If a stain remains after laundering, do not hot-air dry. Treat it with isopropyl alcohol, then sponge with a solution of dishwashing liquid in warm water ¼ teaspoon to ½ cup [1.25–120 ml], and launder in warm water.

❧ Dab the stain with a cloth or cotton swab moistened with isopropyl alcohol—be sure to use a pad of cloth or paper towel underneath the mark to absorb the ink as it runs out of the fabric. Treat resistant ink marks with denatured alcohol.

🌿 In a pinch (i.e., at the office, on vacation, etc.), spray stray ink marks with hair spray (cheap kinds often work best), or blot them with moist baby wipes. If your office supply room has a stash of alcohol pads

Beyond Babies' Bottoms: Baby Wipes vs. Ink

In a clothing store, mark-downs on the tags can mean mark-ups on the merchandise when pens make accidental contact with the clothes. One store manager reports that her staff keeps baby wipes on hand when using ballpoint pens to change prices on garment tags. When an employee in a hurry marks a garment by mistake, a moist wipe takes the ink spot away with equal speed.

used for disinfecting phones and keyboards, apply one of those to your shirt pocket the next time your ink pen goes awry.

On leather:

❧ Rub the mark with a soft cloth dampened with milk, then sponge it with warm water.

On carpet/upholstery:

❧ Dab marks with a cloth or cotton swab moistened with isopropyl alcohol, blotting with clean cloths or white paper towels in between, and changing the cotton swab frequently. Continue until the stain is lifted. Treat persistent stains the same way, using denatured alcohol.

On walls:

❧ Spray ink marks with inexpensive hair spray, or dab them with a cloth or cotton swab dipped in rubbing alcohol. Try denatured alcohol on persistent stains, applying only on the spot and using as little as possible.

On plastic surfaces (such as toys):

❧ That ballpoint tattoo Junior gave his little sister's favorite doll may be almost as tough to remove as a real tattoo. Soak a cotton ball, a piece of cloth, or a paper towel with isopropyl alcohol, and lay it over

Relief for Ink-Stained Desks in Distress

Writer Marie S. of Allentown, Pennsylvania, had ballpoint pens leak on the surface of her white desk. She tried commercial cleaning wipes without success before reaching for plain rubbing alcohol. By rubbing firmly with cloth dampened with alcohol, she was able to remove the ink stains from the painted wood. Marie found that the alcohol also effectively removed ink stains from the case of her notebook computer.

the ink mark, leaving it in place for 15 minutes. Moisten a clean cloth or swab with alcohol, and rub the mark to remove it.

JAMS AND JELLIES

On clothing/washable fabric:

- Scrape up any deposit on the surface and rinse with lukewarm water. Sponge the stain with ¼ teaspoon (1.25 ml) of clear dishwashing liquid in ½ cup (120 ml) of warm water, then rinse with clear water. If a stain persists, treat it as you would a fruit stain; otherwise, launder in warm water.

- Rub glycerin into old or dried jam stains, and leave it on for 30 minutes. Rinse with warm water, then soak the stain in a solution of 1 tablespoon (15 g) of borax in 2 cups (475 ml) of warm water before laundering. Remember that soap sets fruit stains and heat sets sugar stains—avoid both until you're sure the stain is completely gone.

On carpet:

🌿 Scrape or spoon up any material on the surface; blot the stain with lukewarm water, then sponge with 1 teaspoon (5 ml) of clear dishwashing liquid mixed in 1 cup (235 ml) of warm water. Rinse and blot thoroughly with clean cloths or white paper towels. (*See* recommendations for fruit stains on page 102 if a mark remains.)

KETCHUP (ALSO BARBECUE SAUCE, SPAGHETTI SAUCE, AND STEAK SAUCE)

On clothing/washable fabric:

🌿 Gently scrape away any ketchup on the surface, then sponge with cool water, and soak in cold water for at least an hour (overnight for old, dried stains). Stir ¼ teaspoon (1.25 ml) of clear dishwashing liquid into ½ cup (120 ml) of cool water, and blot it onto the stain. Wash as usual in the hottest water recommended by the fabric care label. If a stain remains after laundering, apply a solution of 1 teaspoon (5 ml) of ammonia in ½ cup (120 ml) of cool water, and wash again.

❧ Soak persistent stains in an enzyme solution, following label directions, or make a paste of unseasoned meat tenderizer, and leave it on the spot for 30 minutes. Brush away the paste, and launder as usual.

On carpet:

❧ Clean up any ketchup on the surface, then pour salt over the spot to soak up any remaining material. Spoon up salt that has absorbed the ketchup, and pour on more; repeat until the stain is gone. Vacuum up the remaining salt, and wipe the spot with a damp sponge or cloth.

❧ Blot fresh stains with clear water and white cloths or paper towels. If a spot remains, blot it with a solution of ¼ teaspoon (1.25 ml) of dishwashing liquid in

½ cup (120 ml) of cool water, rinse, and blot dry. If necessary, follow that with 2 tablespoons (28 ml) of ammonia in 1 cup (235 ml) of cool water, blotting on with clean cloths and rinsing with clear water before blotting dry. Treat persistent stains with hydrogen peroxide (test first on a hidden part of the carpet).

MAPLE SYRUP (*SEE* SYRUP, PAGE 131)

MARKER (WASHABLE)
On clothing/washable fabric:

❦ Check the marker manufacturer's recommendations for removal—if they say it's "washable," they should be able to tell you how.

❦ Sponge the stain with cold water until no more color transfers out of the spot. Put a pad of clean cloth or paper towel under the stain, and blot it with a cloth dipped in isopropyl alcohol. Change or reposition the pad under the stain often to avoid restaining the fabric. Launder in the hottest water recommended by the fabric care label, using bleach that's safe for the fabric.

💗 In a pinch, clean up marks with moist baby wipes. Reconsider your choice of car-trip entertainment for the kids.

On carpet:

💗 Blot with cool water, followed by a cloth dampened with isopropyl alcohol (test for colorfastness on a hidden part of the carpet). Change the cloth often to avoid spreading the stain. Continue until the mark is gone; blot with ¼ teaspoon (1.25 ml) of dishwashing liquid in ½ cup (120 ml) of warm water, rinse with clear water, then blot dry with clean cloths.

On appliances, finished wood, hard plastic:

💗 Most hard surfaces should clean up easily with a damp sponge and water. Use a mild abrasive such as baking soda or white toothpaste (not gel) on any remaining marks, rubbing in a circular motion with a damp sponge. Rinse the sponge, and wipe away any residue. Treat persistent stains with isopropyl alcohol or, as a last resort, with nail-polish remover (wipe with clear water in between solvents). Clean up solvent residue with mild dishwashing liquid solution, then wipe clean.

MUSTARD

On clothing/washable fabric:

❧ Treat mustard spills as soon as possible to avoid lasting stains. Scrape or spoon up any surface residue and rinse with cold water. Sponge the spot with ¼ teaspoon (1.25 ml) of clear dishwashing liquid in _ ½ cup (120 ml) of lukewarm water, then launder it in the hottest water recommended by the fabric care label. If a mark remains after washing, treat it with _ ¼ cup (60 ml) of white vinegar in ½ cup (120 ml) of warm water, and wash again. Bleach persistent stains with hydrogen peroxide. Work glycerin into old or dried mustard stains, and leave it on the fabric for 30 minutes before treating as for fresh stains. Heat (from clothes dryer or iron) and alkaline treatments such as ammonia will darken and set mustard stains.

On carpet:

❦ Scrape up surface deposits, working carefully to avoid spreading the spot or forcing it further into the carpet fibers. Sponge with cold water, blotting frequently. Apply glycerin to the stai, and gently work it into the spot; leave it on for 30 minutes. Blot the stain with ¼ teaspoon (1.25 ml) of clear dishwashing liquid in ½ cup (120 ml) of lukewarm water, blot, and rinse with cool water. Blot the stain dry with clean cloths or white paper towels. If it persists, blot with vinegar solution (1 part vinegar to 2 parts warm water), rinse, and blot.

PERFUME AND COLOGNE

On clothing/washable fabric:

❧ Soak up spills immediately and sponge with cool water. Blot with ¼ teaspoon (1.25 ml) of clear dishwashing liquid in ½ cup (120 ml) of warm water, and launder in warm water. If a spot remains, work warm glycerin into the stain, and rinse with cool water. If the stain persists, add 1 tablespoon (15 ml) of white vinegar to 1 cup (235 ml) of water, and blot it on the mark; rinse with cool water. Treat any lingering stain with isopropyl alcohol (test for colorfastness). Dilute 1 part alcohol with 2 parts water if using the solution on acetate; do not apply it to silk or wool fabric.

POLLEN

On fabric:

❧ Don't panic if you find a bright-yellow streak on your Easter outfit after arranging the lilies for the Sunday service—your accidental "pollination" is easily resolved. For starters, say the experts at the Netherlands Flower Bulb Information Center in New York City, resist the urge to brush off the pollen with your hands. The oils on your skin will set the stain, as will wetting the spot or wiping it with a wet cloth. Instead, let the pollen dry, then use a soft brush or a dry facial tissue to brush it away. You also can lift it from your clothes with a piece of sticky tape—just dab it lightly at the pollen until all the pollen is stuck to the tape instead of to your clothing. If any pollen remains, try this "magic" trick: Put the item in direct sunlight for a few hours. The stain should disappear completely.

RED WINE

On clothing/washable fabric:

- Pour or sponge club soda on the stain, and blot with a clean cloth. Continue until the stain is gone or until no more color transfers from the mark onto your blotting cloth. Launder as usual, and check the stain before drying—if it's still evident, sponge with 1 cup (235 ml) of vinegar, 1 tablespoon (15 ml) of clear dishwashing liquid, and ½ cup (120 ml) of water. Let set for 15 minutes; then launder as usual.

🌿 If you have white wine available, pour or sponge it onto the spill to dilute the red wine, then cover the stain with salt, and let it absorb the remaining stain. Shake off the salt, and follow with club soda, then launder as usual.

On linen:

🌿 Place the stained item in a cooking pot, and cover it with milk. Heat the milk to a boil, then take the pot off the burner, and let it set until the stain is gone.

On carpet:

🌿 Dilute the spill with white wine, then flush it with cold water before covering the stain with salt. Let it set for 10 minutes before vacuuming up the salt. Or simply pour ample amounts of club soda over a wine spill, blotting with clean dry cloths until no more color transfers from the stain to the blotter. Repeat until the stain is lifted.

A Speedy Solution for Wine Spills

The lingering stain on a carpet from a red wine spill that didn't come out completely can be enough to make a person swear off their favorite cabernet. Fortunately for wine drinkers (and wine spillers), Evergreen Labs, Inc., of Walla Walla, Washington, makes a nifty product called Wine Away that's formulated to eliminate wine stains on clothing, carpets, and upholstery. Nonwine drinkers can use it too; it takes out other tannin stains, including grape juice and coffee. According to its man-

On marble hearth or countertop:

❧ Pour salt over the stain to prevent it from soaking in. As the salt absorbs the stain, brush it away and apply fresh salt, repeating until the stain is gone. If a stain persists, pour milk over a new application of salt, and let it set for a few hours before wiping with a

ufacturer, Wine Away "is made from fruit and vegetable extracts . . . and contains no bleach. It is nonflammable, biodegradable, and contains no phosphates." Sold in handy spray bottles, Wine Away is easy to use—spray on carpet or upholstery and blot; spray on clothing and launder—and has a pleasant citrus fra-grance. You may find Wine Away on the shelves of your favorite winery or at national retailers of housewares and kitchen supplies; you also can order Wine Away directly from Evergreen Labs through their website (www.wineaway.com) or by calling toll-free (888-946-3292).

damp cloth. You can also use hydrogen peroxide to bleach wine stains on marble surfaces.

On inside of decanter:

🌿 Put white vinegar in a decanter to cover the stains, then fill it with crushed ice and shake or swirl well. Empty the decanter and rinse well. If stains persist, leave vinegar overnight in decanter.

SOFT DRINKS

On clothing/washable fabric:

🌿 Deal with soft drink (colas, root beer, lemonade, etc.) spills as soon as possible, thoroughly rinsing them out of fabric with lukewarm water or club soda. Rinse and blot until you're sure all of the spill is removed, then launder in cool-to-warm (not hot) water. Check for any signs of the stain after washing. If a mark remains, sponge it with ¼ teaspoon (1.25 ml) of clear dishwashing liquid in ½ cup (120 ml) of water with a few drops of ammonia added, and launder again. Do not hot-air dry or iron until the spot is gone; heat will set a stain from any sugary residue that remains on the fabric.

On carpet:

🌿 Soak up the spill, then rinse or sponge the stain with club soda, and blot it with clean rags or white paper towels until no more discoloration is visible. Blot thoroughly with clean cloths, pressing them down firmly for maximum absorption. Treat old, dry soda stains with club soda, too, followed by a solution of ¼ teaspoon (1.25 ml) of clear dishwashing liquid in ¼ cup (60 ml) of warm water with a few drops of ammonia added. Sponge on and blot; rinse with clear water, and blot again. If a stain remains, lighten it with undiluted hydrogen peroxide, dabbed carefully onto the stained area only. Leave it on for 15 minutes, then blot, checking to see that any color you're removing is from the stain and not from your carpet.

On carpet/upholstery:

❧ Cola drinks can leave persistent stains, especially if they dry out before you discover them. If you have Red Erase (www.rederase.com) on hand, give it a try where colas have spilled; old or dried stains may require a couple of applications. Test first on an inconspicuous spot, especially if the manufacturer recommends solvent-based cleaners. (*See* "A Product to Take the Dread Out of Red" on page 166).

SOY SAUCE

On clothing/washable fabric:

❧ Use a clean napkin or paper towel to soak up as much of the spot as possible, then sponge with cool water. Mix 1 tablespoon (15 ml) of white vinegar with 1 cup (235 ml) of lukewarm water, and apply to the stain; rinse and sponge with ¼ teaspoon (1.25 ml) of clear dishwashing liquid in ½ cup (120 ml) of water, and launder in cool water. If there's still a spot after washing, treat with an enzyme cleaner (follow label directions) and wash again.

🌿 Rub glycerin into old or dried soy sauce stains and let it soak in for 30 minutes, then treat as fresh.

🌿 Persistent stains may respond to treatment with isopropyl alcohol, but test for colorfastness first, and dilute the alcohol with an equal amount of water if you're dealing with wool or acetate fabric. Rinse and launder.

SPAGHETTI SAUCE (*SEE* KETCHUP, PAGE 117)

SYRUP

On clothing/washable fabric:

🌿 Gently scrape away or blot up excess syrup from the surface of the fabric. Blot the spot with warm water to remove all of the stickiness, then sponge with mild dishwashing liquid solution (¼ teaspoon [1.25 ml]) mixed in ½ cup [120 ml] of warm water), and wash in warm (not hot) water. Check the spot before drying with a hot-air dryer; if there's any question as to whether the stain has been fully removed, let the item air dry. Soak it in an enzyme cleaner solution, and wash again. If you heat the item (by hot-air drying or ironing) before the syrup is completely gone, the heat may set the sugar stain permanently.

TEA

On clothing/washable fabric:

❦ Blot up the spill, then sponge or rinse the spot with club soda or cold water. If you take your tea with cream, follow the cold water rinsing with hot water, and launder as usual.

❦ Cover wet stains with baking soda to absorb excess moisture; leave in place for at least 15 minutes. Brush or shake off the baking soda, and sponge the stain with a solution of 1 cup (235 ml) of vinegar, 1 tablespoon (15 ml) of dishwashing liquid and ½ cup (120 ml) of water. Let set for 15 minutes; launder as usual.

❧ For durable white and colorfast fabrics, stretch the stained area over a heat-proof bowl or bucket, and secure with a rubber band. Place the bowl in the bathtub or another place where splashing will be contained. Sprinkle borax over the stain to make a thick layer that covers the stain. Carefully pour boiling water around the outer edges of the stain, and circle slowly toward the center of the spot. Repeat as needed to remove all traces of the stain; launder as usual.

On nonwashable fabric:

❧ Treat the stain with a solution made of equal parts isopropyl alcohol and glycerin, then blot with clean cloths or paper towels. Test colorfastness first on a hidden or inconspicuous spot. Repeat treatment as necessary; clean the item according to label instructions.

On upholstery:

❧ Mix 1 tablespoon (15 g) of borax in 2 cups of water, and sponge over the stained area, or combine equal parts warm water and glycerin, and apply to the stain. After either treatment, blot thoroughly with clean, dry cloths or paper towels.

❧ If you have a bottle of Wine Away (www.wineaway.com) in your cleaning cupboard, spray it on the spot, and follow label instructions for stain removal. In addition to wine stains, this water-based product works well on other tannin stains, including coffee and tea. (*See* "A Speedy Solution for Wine Spills" on page 126.)

On carpet:

❧ Soak up excess liquid, then sponge stain with ample amounts of club soda or cold water. If the stain persists, try a solution of 1 teaspoon (5 g) of borax in 1 cup (235 ml) of water, or treat difficult spots with hydrogen peroxide, blotting after 15 minutes. Finish by rinsing with cold water or club soda, then blot thoroughly with clean, dry cloths or paper towels.

🌿 Soak up the spill, then treat with a solution of 1 tablespoon (15 ml) of white vinegar in 1 cup (235 ml) of water with a few drops of dishwashing liquid added. Follow with club soda or clear water, and blot dry.

On marble hearth or countertop:

🌿 Blot up the spill, and pour salt over it to keep it from seeping into the marble. As the salt absorbs the tea, brush it away, and apply fresh salt, repeating until the stain is gone. If it persists, pour milk over a new application of salt, and let set for a few hours before wiping with a damp cloth.

Inside teapot or cups:

🌿 Wet the inside of the teapot or cup with white vinegar. Dip a damp sponge or dishcloth in baking soda or salt, and rub on the inside of the teapot or cup.

Rinse with clear water and wash as usual.

❧ Fill the teapot or cup with water, and toss in a denture-cleaning tablet (use two for a teapot). Let it soak for a few hours before rinsing and washing as usual.

TOMATO (FRESH, CANNED, JUICE/SAUCE/PASTE, SOUP)
On clothing/washable fabric:

❧ Remove any solid material, and blot up liquid spills quickly, taking care to avoid driving the stain into the material. Sprinkle baking soda over liquid spills to absorb the stain, and leave in place for 15 minutes or more. Shake or vacuum away the baking soda, rinse or sponge with cool water, then with equal parts white vinegar and cool water. Rinse again and blot with a solution of ¼ teaspoon (1.25 ml) of clear dishwashing liquid in ½ cup (120 ml) of water; launder in warm water. After washing, check to see if the stain is gone. If the spot persists, soak in an enzyme solution (do not use on silk or wool) for 30 minutes and wash again.

Treat any remaining stain with hydrogen peroxide (test on a hidden or inconspicuous spot first). Avoid setting the stain by applying heat (hot water, hot-air drying, or ironing) until you're sure it's completely gone.

WINE (*SEE ALSO* RED WINE, PAGE 124)

On clothing/washable fabric:

🌿 So much attention is given to treating red wine spills that it's easy to forget that white wine can stain, too, if spills are not handled appropriately. Blot up wine spills, and sponge or rinse with cool water or club soda until all the wine is flushed from the fabric. Wash with detergent in warm (not hot) water; do not use soap. Make sure the spot is gone before hot-air drying or ironing, to avoid setting the sugar stain.

Greasy/Oily Stains

GREASE AND OIL STAINS come from a variety of sources. Motor oil and automotive grease are petroleum-based, for example, while butter and bacon fat have animal origins, and most cooking oils and salad dressings are made of vegetable oils. Whatever the source, greasy and oily stains often are among the most vexing to remove. They tend to soak deeply into porous surfaces and to cling tightly to fabric fibers. If you don't remove them completely, greasy stains also attract and hold dirt and other staining agents. Getting out the grease may be complicated by other stains traveling in their company—dirt and dyes are common companions, while proteins and tannins may be paired with the fats in gravies and some soups.

For washable materials, solving a greasy stain calls for very warm to hot water to counteract the compounds' tendency to solidify, and mild soap or neutral liquid detergent to loosen their hold. With these treatments, most grease and oil stains come out readily in the wash. On other surfaces, absorbents are the place to start. Baking soda, corn starch, fuller's earth, kitty litter, salt, and sawdust may be used to soak up and draw out oily stains from a wide range of materials. Be patient with this process—you may have to apply, sweep up, and reapply an absorbent a few times to get the full benefit, and you may have to leave it in place for several hours. Petroleum-based grease stains may prove tougher than their animal- and vegetable-based cousins, and persistent grease spots may require solvent applications to remove them completely.

In this chapter, you will find solutions for the follow-ing greasy/oily stains:

Butter	Motor oil
Dirty fingerprints	Salad dressing
Grease (automotive)	Smoke and soot
Margarine	Sunscreen/suntan lotion
Marks on walls	Tar

BUTTER

On clothing/washable fabric:

❦ Gently scrape off any solid residue. Sponge the stain with a solution made of ¼ teaspoon (1.25 ml) of clear dishwashing liquid and a few drops of ammonia in ½ cup (120 ml) of warm water. Blot this gently, but firmly, into the spot, then launder as usual in the warmest water recommended for the fabric.

❦ Treat the spot with undiluted glycerin, letting it soak into the fabric, then launder as usual.

On carpet:

🍃 Gently scrape up as much of the butter as possible, taking care to avoid spreading the stain or pushing it further into the carpet fibers. Use white paper towels to blot up as much of the remaining stain as possible. Sponge the spot with a solution of 1–2 tablespoons (15–28 ml) of clear dishwashing liquid in 1 cup (235 ml) of warm water, blotting thoroughly with a clean cloth, and then rinsing with clean water, and blotting again.

DIRTY FINGERPRINTS

On wallpaper:

🍃 Remove the crust from a piece of white bread, and wad the bread into a ball. Gently rub it over dirty spots on wallpaper.

On painted walls:

🍃 Use a clean eraser to gently rub away dirty fingerprints around light switches or other frequently touched spots.

GREASE

On clothing or washable fabric:

❧ Use a dull knife, a spoon, or the edge of a credit card to scrape off as much of the spot as possible from the surface of the fabric. Be gentle to avoid pushing the grease into the fibers. Use white cloths or paper towels to blot up liquid grease stains. Cover the spot with an absorbent, such as salt, baking soda, or fuller's earth. Leave it on the stain as long as necessary to draw the remaining grease out of the fabric. Bear in mind that absorbents aren't much use if the stain is old and dry—in that case, work a small amount of glycerin or petroleum jelly into the spot, and wait 15 minutes before applying an absorbent. Once the absorbent seems to have drawn out as much of the stain as it can, shake or lightly brush it from the fabric, and sponge the remaining mark with a solution of 1 teaspoon (5 ml) of dishwashing liquid in 1 cup (235 ml) of warm water. Launder in the hottest water recommended for the fabric.

If a stain remains, use a clean cloth to blot it with isopropyl alcohol, natural-solvent spot removal products, denatured alcohol, or (as a last resort) acetone-based nail-polish remover (do not use on acetate fabrics). Work in a well-ventilated location when using any of these solvent materials.

On carpet/upholstery and nonwashable fabrics:

Sprinkle an absorbent—fuller's earth, baking soda, salt, or corn starch—over the stain, and brush it lightly into the fibers. Leave it in place for at least an hour before vacuuming or brushing away the absorbent material. Repeat as needed.

For carpets, combine 1 part salt with 4 parts isopropyl alcohol, and blot this onto the stain with a white cloth. Test for colorfastness on a hidden or inconspicuous part of your carpet.

❧ Make a paste of baking soda and water, and rub it on upholstery spots. Leave it to dry before brushing or vacuuming away.

On suede:

❧ Blot the grease with a clean cloth or a white paper towel. Dip a cloth in white vinegar, and sponge the spot. Brush with a suede brush to refresh the nap of the suede.

❧ Treat persistent stains with natural-solvent spot removers, cleaning fluid, or lighter fluid. Test on a hidden part of the suede first, and work in a well-ventilated location.

On concrete patio or wood deck:

❧ Sprinkle salt onto grease drips and spatters on the surfaces around and below your grill. Let set for an hour, then sweep up; reapply as needed. Scrub any lingering spots with warm water and dishwashing liquid, then rinse with clear warm water.

On wallpaper:

❧ Cover grease spots with a paste made from cornstarch and water; let dry, then vacuum or brush away.

❧ Place a piece of plain brown paper (such as the unprinted part of a paper grocery bag) over the stain, and press on the paper with a warm iron. Repeat, moving the paper to clean parts to avoid reapplying the grease to the wallpaper. If any mark remains, dab it carefully with isopropyl alcohol, and blot with a clean cloth.

On book pages:

❧ Rub grease spots with an art gum eraser, then dust with talcum powder or borax. Let set for an hour, and then brush off.

❧ Or, try the ironing method: put a piece of plain (unprinted) brown paper over and under the page, and press with a warm iron. Move the brown paper, and repeat until the grease is removed.

MARGARINE (*SEE* BUTTER, PAGE 141)

MARKS ON WALLS
On painted walls:

❧ Use a clean eraser to gently rub away dirty finger-prints around light switches or other frequently touched spots.

On wallpaper:

❧ Remove the crust from a piece of white bread and wad the bread into a ball. Gently rub it over dirty spots on wallpaper.

MOTOR OIL

On concrete:

❧ Use nonclumping kitty litter to absorb oil spills before they soak in. Leave in place until the litter is saturated; sweep up and repeat if needed. Scrub the stain with a solution of ½ cup (120 ml) of dishwashing liquid in 2 quarts (1.8 L) of warm water with ¼ cup (60 ml) of ammonia added.

❧ Loosen an old oil stain with mineral spirits or paint thinner, letting it soak in for 30 minutes. Cover the spot with nonclumping kitty litter to absorb the stain and the solvent, then scrub with the detergent solution described above. Oil stains that have soaked into the concrete may be permanent.

SALAD DRESSING

On clothing/washable fabric:

❧ Scrape away or blot any material on the surface, working carefully to avoid pushing it into the fabric.

Sprinkle baking soda over the spot to absorb oil from the stain; leave on for a few hours if necessary. Flex the fabric, and shake out the baking soda, then sponge with a mild dishwashing liquid solution (1 teaspoon [5 ml] of clear dishwashing liquid in 1 cup [235 ml] of warm water). Launder in the hottest water safe for the fabric.

SMOKE AND SOOT

On clothing/washable fabric:

❧ Shake out items stained with smoke or soot to get rid of loose particles. Mix 1 teaspoon (5 ml) of clear dishwashing liquid in 1 cup (235 ml) of warm water in a spray bottle; mist affected garments, and saturate visible stains. Launder in the hottest water safe for the fabric; add ½ cup (120 ml) of washing soda to each load to help remove oily residues. If marks remain after washing, dab or blot with a cloth moistened with isopropyl alcohol (after testing first for colorfastness; dilute 1:1 with water on acetate or wool), and wash again.

On carpet:

🌿 Sprinkle salt over sooty spots on carpeting, and leave it on for at least a couple of hours. Vacuum up salt and soot with the attachment hose from your sweeper. Avoid walking on soot-marked carpet or rubbing soot with the vacuum hose; you can press the soot into the fibers, creating oily stains.

Play It Smart with Smoke and Soot

Although smoke and soot may seem similar, they differ in both consistency and how they are deposited. Smoke smells smoky; its fragrance, color, and the nature of any residue it leaves behind depend on its source, while soot has no particular aroma. Soot consists of carbon and oil, typically in a fine dust that lands on surfaces when a furnace malfunctions and releases unburned fuel through your heating system. Smoke residue

As you vacuum soot from household surfaces, clean your vacuum's brush attachment frequently to avoid spreading the problem while you work. Soot stains that remain after vacuuming may require cleanup with a natural-solvent cleaner, a petroleum-based cleaning fluid, or treatment by a cleaning professional.

tends to be concentrated around its source but is carried by heat through cracks and into furniture cushions and carpet pads. Soot distribution tends to be even and superficial—soot gets *on* things rather than in them.

If a fire or a furnace problem leaves you with significant smoke or soot damage in your home, your best bet may be to hire a professional cleaner with experience in removing these substances. The oily nature of soot and the invasive qualities of smoke make each uniquely difficult to remove successfully and completely. Depending on the cause of smoke or soot damage, your homeowner's insurance may cover the costs of professional cleanup.

On stone (around fireplace or woodstove):

🌿 Rub stone surfaces with an art gum eraser to clean off smoke residue.

On brick (around fireplace or woodstove):

🌿 Dip scrub brush bristles in white vinegar, and scrub lightly over brick surfaces to remove smoke residue. Wipe away excess liquid with a damp sponge.

SUNSCREEN/SUNTAN LOTION

On clothing/washable fabric:

🌿 Scrape off and blot any excess material, then cover the spot with an absorbent such as salt, baking soda, fuller's earth, or cornstarch. Wait several hours to allow the absorbent to soak up as much of the oily residue as possible, then shake, brush, or vacuum it away. Sponge the spot with a mild solution of ¼ teaspoon (1.25 ml) of clear dishwashing liquid in ½ cup (120 ml) of warm water, then launder in the warmest water recommended for the fabric. Treat old or lingering spots by rubbing in glycerin, then treating as if fresh.

TAR

On clothing/washable fabric:

❦ Carefully scrape off any surface material, working gently with a lifting motion to avoid spreading the stain or forcing it further into the fabric. Place the stained side of the fabric on a pad of clean cloths or white paper towels, and blot from the underside of the stain with a cotton ball moistened with eucalyptus oil. Reposition the pad as tar leaves the fabric; continue blotting until the stain is removed. Sponge with ¼ teaspoon (1.25 ml) of clear dishwashing liquid in ½ cup (120 ml) of warm water, and launder as usual.

On carpet:

❦ Remove as much of the tar as possible from the surface. If the tar is too soft to remove without spreading the stain, harden the tar by putting an ice-filled plastic bag over the spot until it solidifies. Use a dull knife to scrape off the solidified tar. Combine equal parts glycerin and water, and work it into the spot; leave it on for up to an hour, then use a clean cloth or white paper towels to lift the stain out of the carpet. Repeat as necessary until all the tar is gone. Blot the spot with 1 teaspoon (5 ml) of clear dishwashing liquid in 1 cup (235 ml) of warm water; rinse with clear water, and blot dry.

On vehicles and other impervious surfaces:

❧ Apply linseed oil to tar spots, and leave on for 30 minutes. Moisten a cloth or paper towel with linseed oil, and rub away the spots. Use a clean, dry cloth to wipe up any remaining oil.

Dye Stains

O F THE MAJOR STAIN GROUPS, dyes are probably the most difficult to remove. That's not surprising, since dye stains typically come from sources that are intentionally formulated to permanently retain their bright and/or deeply saturated colors. Since many dye stains come from specific chemical formulations, it's tricky to make a blanket recommendation for their removal as a group. Hot water is typically called for in treating these tough spots, but beware: brightly colored dye stains often travel in the company of sugar (think fruit juices, candy, and powdered drink mixes), so heating these stains might remove the dye but set a brown-yellow sugar stain in its place.

Dye stains may show up in other combinations, too: with grease or oil in cosmetics and crayons, or with protein in flavored gelatin. Your best bet is to treat each of these stains individually and carefully; even so, many dye stains only will come out with the use of solvents or bleaching agents. In this chapter, you will find solutions for the following dye stains:

Candy	Marker (permanent)
Hair dye	Medicine
Ink (felt-tip, fountain pen)	Red stains
Kool-Aid	Shoe polish

CANDY (*SEE ALSO* CHOCOLATE, PAGE 98; AND RED STAINS, PAGE 168)

On clothing/washable fabric:

🖋 Use a dull knife, a credit card, your fingernails, or similar tools to scrape, pluck, or otherwise remove as much of the residue as possible. Soak stained items in warm water, then launder in warm water. Sponge dried stains with a solution of ¼ teaspoon (1.25 ml) of clear dishwashing liquid in ½ cup (120 ml) of warm water before laundering as usual.

🌿 If a red stain remains after an unfortunate candy "incident," treat with Red Erase (www.rederase.com) from Evergreen Labs, Inc. This water-based cleaner is made from fruit and vegetable extracts and is specifically formulated to remove the red stains that seem to go hand-in-hand with kids and the many brightly colored products marketed to them.

On carpet/upholstery:

🌿 Use a dull knife, a credit card, your fingernails, or similar tools to scrape, pluck, or otherwise remove as much of the residue as possible. With a soft, clean cloth, sponge the area with a mild solution of ¼ teaspoon (1.25 ml) of vinegar in 1 cup (235 ml) of warm water. Blot with a fresh cloth, then rinse with clear, warm water, and blot again to remove as much moisture as possible.

Treating a Sweet Spot

"Funny story about that," grinned my son when I asked him about the bright red blotch just below the right rear pocket of his jeans. "Turns out there was a gummy on the seat at lunch today, and I didn't notice it until I got up."

"Get off the furniture," I replied, adding, "And the rug. And get out of those pants." With high-tech tools—my fingernails and a table knife—I scraped and picked away as much of the red gummy stain as I could. At least I didn't have to worry about damaging the fabric—denim is sturdy enough to withstand this sort of abuse (and distressed jeans remain popular with teenagers). Once I'd removed most of the gummy residue from the surface, I was left with a 2- to 3-inch (5.1 to 7.6 cm) reddish smear. I padded the under-side of the stain with a folded white rag and used a second clean white rag (Okay, it was an old athletic sock, turned inside out) to sponge over the spot with lukewarm water. I turned the cloth beneath the stain a few times, as the red coloring moved out of the denim and onto the pad, and kept sponging liberally with water until there was no visible trace of red on either side of the jeans. Then I sponged the area with 1 cup (235 ml) of water with a squirt of dishwashing liquid stirred in, and tossed the jeans into the wash. Washed, dried, and back in his wardrobe, my son's jeans bore no evidence of their close encounter of the sticky kind. Having used nothing more than water, rags, and a little elbow grease, I counted the removal effort a sweet success.

HAIR DYE

On clothing/washable fabric:

❧ The odds of getting out hair dye once it's on fabric are relatively slim. If the dye is from a product you've applied yourself, read the package information to see if it includes instructions for removing any errant dye. If the stain happened while you were getting a professional hair-color treatment, ask your stylist for removal recommendations.

INK (FELT-TIP)

On clothing/washable fabric:

❧ As with ballpoint ink, if you're in possession of the pen that left the mark, use it to spot a sample of similar fabric to find out what treatment works best.

❧ Blot fresh (i.e., wet) felt-tip stains between white cloths or paper towels to remove as much ink as possible. Mix a solution of 1 teaspoon (5 ml) of dishwashing liquid in 1 cup (235 ml) of warm water with a few drops of ammonia added, and carefully dab it on the stain with a cotton swab, using a cloth or paper towel pad under the mark to absorb the ink as it washes out of the spot. Launder as usual. If a stain remains, treat it with isopropyl alcohol or denatured alcohol. Bleach persistent stains with hydrogen peroxide.

Hair Product vs. Hair Product

Keeping in mind that hair dye is made to leave a long-lasting "stain," quick action may save the day if you accidentally get some on your clothing, says hair stylist Randi W. of Allentown, Pennsylvania. Randi soaks spots of errant hair coloring solution with hair spray and finds that this hair-styling product goes a long way toward removing evidence of the other. "I think the alcohol in the hair spray helps keep the [hair] dye from setting," she explains, adding that such stains don't always disappear entirely, even with prompt treatment.

On carpet/upholstery:

✤ Blot freshly applied felt-tip marks with cotton swabs or white paper towels. Dab stains with isopropyl or denatured alcohol, using a cotton swab to treat only the spot.

INK (FOUNTAIN PEN)
On clothing/washable fabric:

✤ Use cool water to rinse away as much of the ink as possible, then blot with ammonia and rinse with cool water. (Dilute ammonia with an equal amount of water for stains on wool or silk; use vinegar to neutralize ammonia if color changes occur). Sponge the remaining stain with 1 teaspoon (5 ml) of clear dishwashing liquid in 1 cup (235 ml) of warm water and launder in warm water. Soak items with old or dried stains overnight in a solution of ½ cup (120 ml) of ammonia in 2 quarts (1.8 L) of water, launder in warm water.

On carpet:

🌿 Sponge the spot with warm water and blot dry. Blot the stain with a solution of ¼ cup (60 ml) of liquid soap in 2 cups (475 ml) of warm water, working it into the spot with a clean cloth. Rinse with warm water, and blot with clean cloths or paper towels; repeat until the stain is lifted, then blot dry.

On leather:

🌿 Act quickly to clean up spills to keep ink from soaking into leather. Moisten a cloth with turpentine, and dab on spots to remove them.

KOOL-AID (*SEE* RED STAINS, PAGE 168)

MARKER (PERMANENT)
On walls:

🌿 Treat fresh marks with a cloth or a sponge that has been dampened with lukewarm water and a teaspoon (5 ml) of dishwashing liquid. Moisten a cloth or cotton ball with isopropyl alcohol, and rub it over any remaining stain, working from the outer edges inward. Hold a clean cloth below the stain as you work to prevent any drips from running down the wall and spreading the stain, or creating cleaning streaks.

❧ Rub persistent stains with a mild abrasive, such as plain white toothpaste (not gel), then wipe clean with a damp sponge. Permanent ink on wallpaper is unlikely to be removed entirely.

On clothing/washable fabric:

❧ Place a clean cloth pad under the stain, and use a cotton swab, a cotton ball, or a clean white cloth to carefully blot denatured alcohol or isopropyl alcohol (test on a hidden area first) on the spot. Reposition the pad and the sponging cloth frequently to avoid reapplying or spreading the stain. Work from the outer edges of the stain inward and, as much as possible, treat only the stain. Blot with alcohol until no more color transfers onto the pad or blotting cloth, then sponge with lukewarm water with a teaspoon of dishwashing liquid added and launder as usual.

It's Called "Permanent" for a Reason

The manufacturers of "permanent" markers are not kidding. Get a stray mark on your skin, and it will wear off fairly quickly; get some on a hard surface, and you may be able to dissolve and scrub it off. Get permanent ink on your clothing, and get used to it. In an utterly unscientific test of the permanence of marker ink, I sacrificed an old white cotton t-shirt. I marked the shirt with three streaks of blue permanent marker, then applied a different solvent to each spot. Of the three solvents I tried, none of them removed the stain entirely, although all three released at least some of the stain from the fabric. I tried two petroleum-based solvents—a lighter-fluid-type product and a lubricant spray—and isopropyl alcohol on the stains, working with a clean cloth pad under each stain, and blotting the

❧ Crayola, the makers of Magic Marker (Permanent) Markers, note on their website (www.crayola.com) that soaking fabrics overnight in hot (105°F.) water and detergent before laundering may remove some of the stain.

product on with another clean cloth. After some initial color-transfer onto the blotting cloths, the petroleum-based solvents left most of the stain intact, plus they made oily spots of their own that called for additional treatment. Repeated blotting with isopropyl alcohol removed almost all of the ink mark, except for the spot where the marker tip rested longest on the fabric. The isopropyl alcohol had the additional advantage of evaporating away, rather than creating a secondary stain. I rinsed the shirt in lukewarm water with a little liquid detergent added, then tossed it in the washer. After laundering, all three ink marks remained almost exactly as they looked when I finished treating them. The isopropyl alcohol was the clear winner in my test, but I wouldn't call it a total success. It removed enough of the stain to save a casual garment that was marked in a fairly inconspicuous spot, but not nearly enough to rescue a white or light-colored dress shirt or blouse.

MEDICINE (*SEE* RED STAINS, BELOW)

RED STAINS (SOFT DRINKS, SPORTS DRINKS, FLAVORED GELATIN, MEDICINE, CANDY)

On clothing/washable fabric:

🌿 Flush the spill right away with club soda, and blot with a clean cloth; repeat until the stain is gone. If you don't have club soda, use cold water.

They Cure Parental Pain, Too

Look for dye-free formulations of popular over-the-counter medications for children and avoid the risk of a having a cherry-red stain to clean up. It's a small way to reduce the stress you're already feeling when nursing a sick child who might not want to take his medicine.

Act quickly to neutralize the stain by sponging it with 1 tablespoon (15 ml) of ammonia in a cup of water. Blot, rinse with clear cool water, blot again, and repeat until the stain is removed. Launder in cool water with a bleach safe for the fabric.

On carpet:

Quick action is needed with red spills to keep them from soaking into carpet padding and becoming permanent parts of your décor.

Blot up the spill to keep it from spreading, then flush the stain with club soda. Use clean cloths or white paper towels to soak up liquid and color, pour on more club soda, and continue rinsing and blotting until the stain is removed or no more color transfers out of the spot onto your blotting cloths. If you're left with a spot, soak it with hydrogen peroxide or lemon juice, and let it set for 15 minutes. Blot and assess—is the stain gone or at least getting lighter? If it's working on the stain without taking the color out of your carpet, continue until the spot is vanquished or sufficiently inconspicuous.

A Product to Take the Dread Out of Red

The bright red food dye that makes fruit punch, sports drinks, and candy so tempting to kids seems to have an almost magnetic attraction to white and light-colored clothing, carpet, and upholstery. What parent hasn't shaken in fear at the sight of a child climbing into the car with a red lollipop clutched firmly in his fist? Who hasn't restricted their children's access to certain furnishings–or even entire rooms–whenever red fruit punch is being served? It's not just paranoia; those brilliant red foods and drinks (as well as red markers) create stains that are tough, if not impossible, to remove, especially if you're trying to avoid resorting to harsh cleansers, solvents and bleaches.

There's good news, though, for parents and kids, in the form of Red Erase, a citrus-scented, spray-on treatment specifically

❦ Blot up the spill, and apply a solution of 1 tablespoon (15 ml) of ammonia in 1 cup (235 ml) of water to the spot as soon as you can to prevent the dye from set-

formulated to get the red out. Made by Evergreen Labs, Inc. of Walla Walla, Washington, Red Erase is "a water-based product made from fruit and vegetable extracts" and is "perfectly safe for use around children and pets," say the manufacturers, who got their start in the stain-removal business with a similar product called Wine Away (*see* "A Speedy Solution for Wine Spills" on page 126). While Wine Away is good for treating fruit juice spots, as well as red wine stains, Red Erase is formulated specifically to do the trick on those cherry red spots that seem to follow kids everywhere. You can order 2-ounce (60 ml) and 12-ounce (355 ml) spray bottles of Red Erase directly from Evergreen Labs via their website (www.rederase.com) or by calling 888-946-3292. Don't let the name limit your stain-removal efforts: Red Erase takes out stains of other colors, too. According to the manufacturer, Red Erase effectively treats cola and coffee stains, and I used it to get rid of an herbal tea stain, as well as stains made by orange, purple, pink, and bright green candy.

ting on your carpet. Cover the stain with table salt to soak up the stain. Leave the salt in place for 10–15 minutes to soak up the stain before vacuuming it away. Repeat as needed; rinse with clear water, and blot dry.

SHOE POLISH

On clothing/washable fabric:

- Carefully scrape off any surface deposit, then place the stained fabric spot-side-down on cloth or a paper-towel pad and sponge the back of the spot with 1 teaspoon (5 ml) of clear dishwashing liquid in ½ cup (120 ml) of warm water. Reposition the pad frequently as color transfers out of the mark; continue until the spot is removed or no more color leaves the stain. For colored fabrics, combine 1 part isopropyl alcohol with 2 parts water, and blot on persistent stains (test first on an inconspicuous part of the item); use undiluted isopropyl alcohol on white fabrics. Rinse with clear water once the stain is lifted, and launder as usual.

On carpet/upholstery:

❧ Carefully scrape or blot up any material on the surface, taking care to avoid spreading the polish or forcing it deeper into the fibers of your carpet or upholstery. Moisten a cloth with isopropyl alcohol, and sponge over the stain, blotting and repeating until it is removed. Test isopropyl alcohol on a hidden or inconspicuous place first, to make sure it doesn't cause dyes to run. Persistent stains may require the same treatment with denatured alcohol. Once the stain has been removed, sponge clear water on the area, then blot with a solution of ¼ teaspoon (1.25 ml) of clear dishwashing liquid in ½ cup (120 ml) of warm water; rinse with clear water, and blot dry with clean cloths or white paper towels. Avoid carpeted areas and upholstered furnishings next time you polish your shoes.

Combination and Other Stains

WHILE SOME STAINS fall neatly into a category such as tannin or grease, many of the spots and marks you encounter will be "combination" stains. Food stains, for example, are as varied as the things we eat and drink; A dropped bite of chicken parmesan may create a combination protein, grease, and tannin stain, while spilled coffee with cream and sugar leaves a spot that's made of tannin, protein, and sugar. As such, these stains require a variety of removal techniques.

While you might classify a food stain by its major components—steak, protein; coffee, tannin; candy, dye—the truth is that the majority of food stains are a combination of elements, each of which may need a separate treatment for successful stain removal.

Combination stains can prove to be tricky, since the first treatment for one element of a spot may be the thing that sets another component of the stain. However, there is a gentle, effective, and widely available product that removes a wide range of food stains reasonably well: dishwashing liquid. For treating combination food stains on washable fabrics (including carpet and upholstery), look for a clear or white liquid dishwashing detergent that's not packed with additives such as fragrances or skin-softeners. Avoid soaps, which will set fruit stains. Simply mix a mild solution of dishwashing liquid in cool-to-lukewarm water, and sponge it on food-related spots. Use clear water to rinse the solution from carpeting or upholstery, toss treated clothing in the washer, and launder as usual. This solution makes a good laundry pretreatment, too.

In addition to the four main stain groups and combination stains, there are a few other common types of stains: adhesives; minerals and oxidation; paints and lacquers; and physical damage. As with the other groups of stains, similar treatments may apply to some or all of the stains within each of these smaller categories.

In this chapter, you will find solutions for the following combination and "other" stains:

COMBINATION STAINS

Candle wax (colored candles: grease/oil and dye)

Cosmetics (dye and grease/oil)

Crayon (grease/oil and dye)

Cream soup (may be protein, grease/oil, and tannin)

Gravy (grease/oil and protein)

Greasy dirt (grease/oil and tannin)

Lipstick (grease/oil and dye)

Makeup (grease/oil and dye)

OTHER STAINS

ADHESIVES
Chewing gum
Glue (permanent)
Stickers/decals

PAINTS AND LACQUERS
Nail polish
Paint

MINERALS AND OXIDATION
Chalk
Hard-water deposits
Iodine
Mud
Pencil
Rust/minerals
Tarnish

PHYSICAL DAMAGE
Bleach
Burn marks
Mildew
Mystery stains and marks
Scorch marks
Scuff/skid marks
Water stains/marks

Combination Stains

CANDLE WAX (COLORED CANDLES)

On clothing/washable fabric:

🌿 Apply a plastic bag filled with ice to the wax to freeze it, or simply toss the item into the freezer. Once the wax is cold and brittle, flex the fabric to break away as much wax as possible, then lift and scrape away any remaining residue with a dull knife. The more wax you remove this way, the better, but use care to avoid pressing the stain deeper into the fabric. Place absorbent material above and below the stain—unprinted pieces of brown paper grocery bags or white paper towels or paper napkins work well—and press over the area with a warm iron (medium setting). Move or replace the brown paper above and below the stain to avoid respotting the fabric, and continue pressing with the iron until no more wax transfers onto the paper.

❧ Next, use a clean cloth to rub vegetable oil on the stain. Use a white paper towel to wipe up any excess oil, then launder as usual.

❧ Blot the stain with a cloth dipped in denatured alcohol to remove any remaining wax and any color left on the fabric. Launder as usual.

❧ Treat the remaining spot with a natural solvent cleaner before laundering. Use dishwashing liquid or liquid laundry detergent in warm water to sponge solvent spots before laundering as usual.

❧ If the stain persists, apply hydrogen peroxide (test on a hidden spot first), and let it set for 15 minutes before blotting with a clean cloth. Repeat until the stain is gone, then rinse with clear water, and wash again.

On carpet/upholstery:

❧ Treat the same as on clothing, but without placing absorbent material over and under the stain. Use a plastic bag filled with ice to freeze the wax until it's brittle, then use a dull knife (or a credit card) to scrape up and off as much as you can. Put a piece of unprinted brown paper bag or white paper towels or napkins over the spot, and press with a warm iron, moving the paper as it absorbs the wax. Keep with it until no more wax transfers onto the paper.

🌿 Blot any remaining stain with a clean cloth that has been moistened with denatured alcohol (test in an inconspicuous spot first).

🌿 Treat with natural solvent cleaner (test first!), by dampening a cloth with it and blotting it onto the stain. Do not apply solvent directly to carpets, as it may damage the backing. Blot thoroughly with clean cloths or paper towels to remove residue.

On finished wood:

🌿 Use a credit card, dull knife, or similar tool to scrape off as much wax as possible without damaging the wood. Use a blow-dryer to soften any remaining wax, then wash it off with a cloth dipped in Murphy's Oil Soap in warm water. Wipe dry with a soft cloth, then polish.

COSMETICS (*SEE* LIPSTICK, PAGE 189; OR MAKEUP, PAGE 190)

CRAYON

On finished (paint, stain, varnish) surfaces:

❦ Spray crayon marks with WD-40, and wipe away with a soft cloth. To clean up any residue from this treatment, moisten a sponge with a solution of ¼ teaspoon (1.25 ml) of dishwashing liquid in a cup of warm water and wipe. Repeat as needed, then rinse the sponge in clear water, and wipe the surface a final time.

On wallpaper:

❦ Rub marks very gently with a dry steel wool pad.

❦ Try a mild abrasive, such as baking soda or white toothpaste (not gel). Sprinkle baking soda on a damp sponge, and gently rub it over the marks, or coat them with a small amount of white toothpaste and rub lightly with a damp sponge or cloth. Rinse your sponge in clear water, and wipe away any residue.

On clothing/washable fabric:

❧ Put a pad of cloth or paper towels under the stain, and spray the spot with WD-40. Turn the item over, and spray the other side of the mark. Wait a few minutes, then dab dishwashing liquid on the spot, and work it in. Change or refold the padding under the stain as it transfers out of the fabric. Launder in the warmest water recommended by the fabric's care label; use all-fabric bleach if appropriate.

On carpet/upholstery:

❧ Use a spoon or a dull knife to scrape any crayon off the surface. Spray marks with WD-40, and leave it on for a few minutes. Loosen the stain with a small, stiff bristle brush (such as a clean toothbrush), and blot with paper towels. Spray again with WD-40, then dab dishwashing liquid on the spot. Use the brush to "work" the stain again, then wipe with clean, damp sponge or cloth. Repeat this process until the stain is gone.

On concrete:

- Spray marks with WD-40, then brush with a stiff scrub brush. Spray again to further loosen the stain, and wipe with cloth or paper towels. Repeat until the stain is gone.

CREAM SOUP

On clothing/washable fabric:

- Blot up excess liquid, and use a spoon or dull knife to scrape up any solid material. Sponge with cool water to remove as much of the stain as possible, then soak the item in cool water a few hours. After soaking, add ¼ teaspoon (1.25 ml) of clear dishwashing liquid and a few drops of ammonia to ½ cup (120 ml) of warm water, and blot onto the spot with a clean cloth, pressing it into the stain without rubbing. Launder as usual in the warmest water recommended by the fabric care label.

Meet the Maker

Struggling with a thorny stain caused by a product? Check the label to see if it lists the manufacturer's website, or fire up your favorite search engine and watch the "hits" add up. Increasingly, companies are using the Internet to provide their customers with the kind of information that used to be available from a single, harried customer service rep during "normal business hours," if at all.

Crayola, the maker of crayons and dozens of other art and craft supplies, provides a great example of this. At its website, www.crayola.com, you can find stain-removal recommendations for every product the company makes.

Because product formulations—even for common products like blue ballpoint ink pens—often vary from one manufacturer to the next, and since companies may change a product's content over the years, last year's tried-and-true removal method may not work today. Get up-to-date recommendations on the Web; if your cyber-stain-seach comes up short, use the manufacturer's website to seek advice via email—most online customer service inquiries yield a response within 24 hours.

On carpet/upholstery:

🍃 Blot the spill with white cloths or paper towels, and scrape or spoon up any solid material. Mix a solution of 1 part dishwashing liquid to 4 parts lukewarm water and sponge on the stain with a cloth. Rinse by blotting with a cloth dipped in clean water, then blot with a clean, dry towel. Repeat until the stain is gone. For persistent spots, blot with a solution of 2 tablespoons (28 ml) of ammonia in 1 cup (235 ml) of water; rinse and blot dry.

GRAVY

On clothing/washable fabric:

🍃 Blot up excess liquid, and use a spoon or dull knife to scrape up any solid material. Sponge the spot with cool water to remove as much of the stain as possible, then soak the item in cool water a few hours. After soaking, add ¼ teaspoon (1.25 ml) of clear dishwashing liquid and a few drops of ammonia to ½ cup (120 ml) of warm water, and blot onto the spot with a clean cloth, pressing it into the stain without rubbing. Launder as usual in the warmest water recommended by the fabric care label.

❧ Loosen old, dry stains with glycerin, then treat as above.

On carpet/upholstery:

❧ Blot the spill with white cloths or paper towels, and scrape or spoon up any solid material. Mix a solution of 1 part dishwashing liquid to 4 parts lukewarm water, and sponge on the stain with a cloth. Rinse by blotting with a cloth dipped in clean water, then blot with a clean, dry towel. Repeat until the stain is gone. For persistent spots, blot with a solution of 2 tablespoons (28 ml) of ammonia in 1 cup (235 ml) of water; rinse and blot dry.

GREASY DIRT

On clothing/washable fabric:

🌿 Sponge with a solution of 1 teaspoon (5 ml) of dish-washing liquid in 1 cup (235 ml) of warm water. For persistent stains, make a paste by adding water to washing soda, and spread over the spot. Let it dry, brush off the paste, and launder as usual in the hottest water recommended by the fabric care label.

What Is Greasy Dirt?

Along with grass stains, greasy dirt is often found on the knees of kids' jeans, the result of a fall on that surface known as black-top, asphalt, or macadam. Greasy dirt stains also result from puddle-jumping on paved surfaces—the water in such puddles effectively disperses the soil in solution, along with the accumulated oil that floats on top.

LIPSTICK

On clothing/washable fabric:

◉ Rub with a wet bar of soap; launder as usual.

◉ Treat the spot with undiluted glycerin, then launder as usual.

◉ Sponge the stain with a cloth moistened with isopropyl or denatured alcohol, then rub a small amount of clear dishwashing liquid on the spot. Launder as usual.

◉ In a pinch, shaving cream (not shaving gel) can be a good solvent for lipstick stains. Work a dab of it into the spot, then rinse with club soda or cold water before laundering as usual.

◉ Lipstick leaves a persistent stain that can be nearly impossible to remove from fabrics. Solvent-type cleaning fluids work best on lipstick stains; look for a natural solvent product. Seek professional help in removing lipstick marks from expensive garments.

MAKEUP

On clothing/washable fabric:

❧ Use a slice of bread to wipe or brush away makeup smudges on dark-colored clothing.

❧ Wet a cloth with white vinegar, wring it out, and use it to wipe away makeup spots on clothing.

❧ Sponge the stain with a cloth moistened with denatured alcohol, then rub a small amount of dishwashing liquid on the spot. Launder as usual.

❧ In a pinch, shaving cream (not shaving gel) can be a good solvent for cosmetic stains. Work a dab of it into the spot, then rinse with club soda or cold water before laundering as usual.

On carpet:

❧ Use paper towels to soak up as much of the stain as possible, then rinse thoroughly with club soda or cold water, sponging and blotting repeatedly. Make a solution of ¼ cup (60 ml) of clear dishwashing liquid in 2 quarts (1.8 L) of cool water, and sponge over the stain, blotting frequently. Rinse with cool water, and blot some more. If you still have a stain, apply undiluted hydrogen peroxide, and leave it on for 15 minutes before blotting with clean cloths or paper towels. Repeat until the stain is gone or rendered adequately inconspicuous, then rinse with club soda or cold water, and blot dry.

❧ In a pinch, shaving cream (not shaving gel) can be a good solvent for cosmetic stains. Work a dab of it into the spot, then rinse with club soda or cold water before laundering as usual.

🌿 Cosmetics, especially waterproof products, may create persistent stains that are nearly impossible to remove. It may take a solvent to lift some cosmetic stains. Look for a natural solvent product, or call a professional carpet cleaner.

Other Stains—Adhesives

CHEWING GUM

On clothing/washable fabric:

🌿 Freeze the gum by placing the garment in a plastic bag, such as a grocery bag in the freezer, and pressing the bag into the gum. Leave in the freezer for at least an hour, until the gum is completely frozen and brittle. Remove from the freezer, and grasp the gum through the side of the bag. Gently pull the gum away from the fabric, taking care not to damage the fibers. Depending on how much gum remains, the rest of the removal process may be a tedious task. If the fabric can take it, scrape the residue with a dull knife, a spoon, or a credit card, using a lifting motion and stopping frequently to shake off any crumbs you've loosened. Don't scrape too hard, or you'll replace the gum spot with a hole. If scraping's not an option, pluck the rest of the gum off or out of the fabric with your fingernails, then dab the spot with ¼ teaspoon (1.25 ml) of dishwashing liquid in ½ cup (120 ml) of warm water, and launder as usual. If the gum is firmly embedded in the fabric, you may need to apply a natural-solvent spot remover to loosen the stain. Work in a well-ventilated area when using such products, and follow label instructions closely.

On carpet/upholstery:

⚘ If the gum is soft, scrape up as much as possible using a putty knife, credit card, or similar tool; take care to avoid spreading the gum further. Fill a zip-closure plastic bag with ice, and place it over the gum, leaving it in place until the gum is frozen and brittle. When the gum is hardened, scrape and pluck away as much of it as you can. Dab petroleum jelly on any gum that remains, and scrape some more. Finally, use natural-solvent spot remover on a clean cloth to remove the last bits of residue, following label directions.

Sugary vs. Sugar-free

No matter what dentists recommend for their patients who chew gum, the sugar-laden types that are worse for your teeth are better if you have to disengage them from your clothing or carpet. For starters, sugar-free gum doesn't freeze in a normal household freezer. After a night in my freezer, a blob of regular (with sugar) chewing gum was brittle and hardened, which made it easy to break it into pieces that I could peel off of the fabric they were stuck to. But a blob of sugar-free gum, stuck to the same kind of fabric, remained almost as pliable as when it when into the freezer. There was

On shoes:

🍂 Place the gummy shoe inside a plastic shopping bag, and press the bag into the gum. Put the bagged shoe in the freezer for an hour or longer to harden the gum. Remove the bag from the freezer, and grasp the gum through the outside of the bag. Pull the shoe out of the bag while pulling as much gum away from

no chance of breaking it up, and it was no easier to remove from the fabric than when it was fresh.

If you know the gum on your rug is sugar-free, skip the ice bag, and bring the heat. Use a blow-dryer set on high to warm, and soften the sticky stuff, heating it for about a minute. Keep the dryer at least 6 inches away from the rug to avoid melting or scorching the fibers. Then scrape/pluck up the softened gum, reheating as necessary with the blow-dryer. Once you've gotten most of it, dab a small amount of petroleum jelly onto the remaining residue, and work it in. Then heat once more, and pluck out any gum that's still visible. Sponge the spot with 1 teaspoon (5 ml) of dishwashing liquid in 1 cup (235 ml) of warm water, blot with a clean cloth, then rinse with clear water and blot again.

the shoe as you can. Most of it should stick to the bag rather than your shoe.

❦ Spray any remaining gum residue with WD-40, and let it soak in for a minute. Use a paper towel to wipe away the gum and lubricant spray.

On hard surfaces:

❦ Put a plastic bag filled with ice over the gum to harden it. Use a putty knife, credit card, or similar tool to scrape away the entire blob. If any stain remains, wipe it with a paper towel moistened with vegetable oil, then use a mild solution of dishwashing liquid in water to finish the cleanup.

GLUE (PERMANENT)

On hard surfaces:

❦ For best results, check the manufacturer's instructions for safe removal. Cyanoacrylate (a.k.a. "super") glues may be dissolved with acetone-based nail-polish remover. Ventilate the area, and keep away from heat sources or open flames.

On skin:

❧ Loosen glued fingers by wetting with warm, soapy water and gently rubbing glued surfaces together. Do not pull.

❧ Or use a cotton swab to apply acetone-based nail-polish to the affected area. Ventilate to minimize fume inhalation; avoid heat sources and open flames. Once the fingers are freed, flush them with clear water, and wash thoroughly with mild soap and water.

On clothing/washable fabric:

❧ Permanent glues may be impossible to remove from fabrics without damage. Consult the manufacturer's website or customer service hotline for product-specific recommendations. Use isopropyl alcohol, acetone-based nail-polish remover, or denatured alcohol sparingly and with extreme caution, as any of these products may cause fabric dyes to run. Follow all usual precautions when working with volatile solvents. Do not use on acetate, nylon, silk or wool.

Stuck on Stickers?

Stickers seem like the last safe resort for teachers seeking minor rewards for their students. Brightly colored and available in an endless variety of shapes and themes, stickers carry no worries about food allergies, dental damage from sugary sweets, childhood obesity, etc.–and kids love them! Kids' doctors and dentists get plenty of mileage from these adhesive honors, too, using them to reward good behavior or to mark the timing of a fluoride treatment. It's fun to see your child festooned with colorful stickers, and few things seem less likely to cause a parent worry. Until you launder a sticker, that is.

A few years ago, I missed a sticker on my son's shirt while doing the laundry. It wasn't until the shirt had been through the washer and the dryer that I realized my lapse. The colorful, paper part of the sticker had disappeared into

STICKERS/DECALS

On clothing/washable fabric:

🌿 Pluck off as much of the adhesive as possible, taking care to avoid rubbing it further into the fabric. Work

tiny colorful bits that wound up in the lint trap, leaving only a firmly attached (heat-sealed) patch of adhesive on the front of the shirt. Even that was barely visible, so I put the shirt back in my son's drawer. The next time he wore it, things got worse: the lingering adhesive was a magnet for dirt, lint, and everything else. Now it was a dirty, sticky patch. I tried a commercial laundry pretreatment, which removed the soil, but not the sticky. Frustrated, I put the shirt aside and forgot about it. Time passed, and the shirt, now the right size for my younger son, caught my eye. So did the sticky spot. Figuring that I'd either "cure it or kill it," I reached for a bottle of orange-oil solvent and found that it had label instructions for treating stains on clothing. I put a pad of white rags under the stain and squirted on a bit of the orange-oil solvent, then blotted with another white rag. And, after more than two years' time, the sticky spot was gone. With laundering, the shirt showed no signs of its long-standing relationship with the sticker.

a small amount of vegetable oil into the remaining residue, and scrape with a spoon or a dull knife to lift it off the fabric. Once the sticky stuff is lifted, sponge the area with 1 cup (235 ml) of warm water mixed with 1 teaspoon (5 ml) of dishwashing liquid to remove the vegetable oil. Rinse thoroughly, and launder as usual. For sticky spots that have been set by heat and or time, apply an orange-oil solvent product to the spot, following label directions, then apply mild dishwashing liquid solution to remove any residue from the solvent; rinse and launder.

On finished wood:

❧ Carefully peel away as much of the sticker as possible without scratching or gouging the surface. Dip a soft, clean cloth in vegetable oil, and use it to saturate the rest of the sticker with vegetable oil. Let it soak for a few minutes, then use the cloth to rub gently over the spot until the sticker (and any associated stickiness) is removed completely. If removal still proves difficult, apply more vegetable oil to the sticky spot, and let it soak for up to an hour before wiping again with a soft cloth. Wipe up any oil residue with a clean cloth.

Other Stains—Minerals and Oxidation

CHALK

On clothing/washable fabric:

❧ If the chalk is dry, remove as much as possible by shaking, vacuuming, or carefully brushing with a soft brush, a dry microfiber dust cloth, or even a dry paper towel. Do not brush with your bare hands (unless you have no other option), since the oils on your skin can help to set a dry stain like chalk.

❧ If a colored stain remains after you've removed as much dry residue as possible, put a cloth or paper towel pad beneath the stain, and use a clean cloth to blot on isopropyl alcohol. Change the pad under the spot and the blotting cloth frequently until no more color comes out of the stain. Once the stain is gone, blot the area with a solution of ¼ teaspoon (1.25 ml) of clear dishwashing liquid in ½ cup (120 ml) of warm water, and launder as usual.

HARD-WATER DEPOSITS
On tub and shower walls:

❦ Spray shower walls and tub surfaces with hot, undiluted white vinegar—heat it on the stove or in a microwave until it's hot, but not too hot to work with. Leave it on for 15 minutes, then scrub with a scrubbing sponge moistened with vinegar. Spray on more hot vinegar as needed; rinse with clear warm water when finished, and wipe dry.

Around drains:

❦ Rub deposits around drains with a cut lemon.

IODINE

On clothing/washable fabric:

🌿 Blot stains with soap and warm water, rinse, then launder if the mark is gone. Dab remaining stain with isopropyl alcohol; if a spot remains, launder with a bleach that's safe for the fabric.

🌿 Moisten fresh iodine spots with warm water, and place the item in the sunlight, or hold it over the steam from a boiling kettle; in a few minutes the stain will be gone. Launder as usual.

Be a "Squeegee Whiz"

If you take a minute after showering to wipe down the walls with a squeegee, you'll reduce the buildup of hard-water deposits on the shower walls, while also reducing the humid conditions that contribute to mildew growth.

MUD

On clothing/washable fabric:

❧ Here's the rare stain that can and should wait for treatment. Let mud dry before you try to remove it. Brush or vacuum dried mud stains thoroughly before you even think about wetting them. Sponge any remaining marks with ¼ teaspoon (1.25 ml) of clear dishwashing liquid in ½ cup (120 ml) of warm water with a few drops of ammonia added, then launder in warm water. If any stain remains after washing, blot it with a cloth dipped in isopropyl alcohol (test colorfastness on a hidden part of the garment first). Red earth stains may need to be treated as rust stains (*see* Rust/Minerals, page 206).

On carpet/upholstery:

❧ Pour salt or baking soda over wet mud spots, and let them dry completely. Vacuum up salt or baking soda and dried soil, brushing gently if necessary to loosen the soil from the carpet fibers. If any mark remains, sponge with solution of ¼ teaspoon (1.25 ml) of dish-washing liquid in ½ cup (120 ml) of warm water with a few drops of ammonia added. Stains from red soil may require the same treatment as for rust stains.

On suede:

❧ Let mud dry completely and brush/vacuum it up. Use a suede brush, a suede cleaning block, or a clean white eraser to brush away any remaining traces.

PENCIL

On clothing/washable fabric:

❧ Gently brush or vacuum dry pencil marks to remove any loose residue; carefully rub the spot with a clean art gum eraser to lift more of the mark. Mix 1 tea-spoon (5 ml) of clear dishwashing liquid and a few drops of ammonia in 1 cup (235 ml) warm water, and rub this solution into the spot before laundering in warm water.

On hard surfaces:

🌿 Use mild detergent solution to wipe pencil marks off nonporous surfaces. Apply a clean art gum eraser to rub off marks on wallpaper, unfinished wood, and painted walls.

RUST/MINERALS

On clothing/washable fabric:

🌿 Rub a paste of salt and vinegar into rust stains, and let set for 30 minutes before laundering as usual. Or mix the salt with lemon juice instead of vinegar, and place in the sun to dry before washing. You also can drip lemon juice onto salt covering the stain and then hold the spot over steam. Rinse and repeat as needed. If the fabric will tolerate it, top the stain with a mixture of lemon juice and salt, leave it on for a few minutes, then stretch the stained fabric over a heat-proof bowl and secure with a rubber band. Set the bowl in a bathtub, and carefully pour boiling water through the stain.

꧁ Or, combine the bleaching powers of lemon juice and sunlight to wipe out a rust stain. Dab undiluted lemon juice on rust spots, and place the garment in the sun for a few hours; launder as usual.

꧁ Cream of tartar is another rust remover you might find in your kitchen cupboard. Cover the spot with cream of tartar, then gather the fabric around the

Don't Reach for the (Chlorine) Bleach

Bypass the chlorine bleach when treating rust stains—it's more likely to make them worse (i.e., darker) instead of making them disappear. If your water is rich in iron and minerals, best to leave chlorine bleach off the laundry list, too.

stain to form a little "pouch" with the cream of tartar inside. Dip the "pouch" in hot water for about 5 minutes; launder as usual.

On porcelain tub/sink:

❧ Remove light rust stains by rubbing them with the inside of a freshly cut lemon.

❧ Sprinkle cream of tartar on your sponge or directly on stains and scour them away—like baking soda, cream of tartar is a mild abrasive.

❧ For a little more stain-fighting power, make a paste by mixing 3 tablespoons (43 g) of cream of tartar with 1 tablespoon (15 ml) of hydrogen peroxide. Spread on stains and scrub, then rinse with clear water. If stains persist, spread on the cream of tartar-peroxide paste, add a couple drops of ammonia, and leave on the spot for 2 hours before scrubbing. Rinse with clear water.

On stainless steel sink:

ᘒ Wipe rust spots with a sponge moistened with undiluted vinegar, or coat them with a paste of 3 parts cream of tartar to 1 part hydrogen peroxide. Let the paste dry; wipe away with a damp sponge.

On fixtures:

ᘒ Rub away rust stains with a paste of salt and lemon juice. Rinse with clear water, and polish with a soft cloth.

On toilet bowl:

ᘒ Flush toilet to wet sides of the bowl, then rub on a paste of borax and lemon juice. Leave on the stains for 2 hours before scrubbing well and rinsing.

On countertops:

ᘒ Dab rust spots with white toothpaste (not gel), and rub with a damp sponge until the stain is gone; rinse with clear water, and wipe dry.

❧ Moisten cream of tartar with hydrogen peroxide or lemon juice to make a paste, spread it over rust stains, and leave on for 30 minutes. Scrub and rinse; repeat as needed until stains are removed.

On pots:

❧ Clean lime deposits (whitish buildup) from pots or wood stove steamers. Fill with water and add a few tablespoons (45–60 ml) of vinegar and half of a fresh lemon, cut into slices. Boil for 15 minutes, then let cool; empty the contents, scrub the pot, rinse, and wipe dry.

On knives or other kitchen utensils:

❧ Use an onion to clean the rust from kitchen knives and other utensils. Stick a rusty blade into an onion and leave for an hour; wiggle the blade now and then to help the process. After an hour, remove the blade, wash, and dry. If the rust is still present, stick the blade back into the onion for another hour.

On tools:

❧ Combine 2 tablespoons (28 g) of salt and 1 tablespoon (15 ml) of lemon juice in a paste, and rub on rusty spots with a dry cloth. Rinse away the paste and dry thoroughly. Once your tools are rust-free, clean and dry, dampen a cloth with a penetrating lubricant, such as WD-40, and wipe on a thin, protective layer to prevent rust from recurring.

On car chrome:

❧ Crumple aluminum foil into a ball, and rub it over rust spots until they're gone.

On slate:

❧ Pour undiluted white vinegar on rust stains, and scrub with a stiff-bristle brush. Rinse with clear water once stains are removed.

On concrete:

🌿 Wet rust stains with undiluted white vinegar or lemon juice, and cover with plastic to keep from drying. Let set for 15 minutes, uncover and scrub with a stiff-bristle brush. Rinse thoroughly with clear water.

TARNISH

On brass, bronze, or copper:

🌿 Combine 1 tablespoon (15 g/ml) each of salt, flour, and vinegar to make a paste. Use a damp cloth to rub this mixture onto tarnished surfaces. Wash, rinse, and wipe dry.

🌿 Dip the cut edge of a lemon half in salt, and rub over tarnished surfaces, then wash, rinse, and wipe dry.

🌿 Wipe ketchup or Worcestershire sauce on tarnished surfaces, and rub until the tarnish is gone, then wash, rinse, and wipe dry.

On silverware and silver jewelry:

❧ Rub salt on tarnished spots, then wash and wipe dry.

❧ Tear strips of aluminum foil and lay them on the bottom of a heat-proof, nonmetallic bowl. Put silver items on top of the foil, and pour 1 to 3 quarts (946 ml–2.8 L) of boiling water over them (enough to cover completely). Add 1 teaspoon (5 g) of salt and 1 teaspoon (5 g) of baking soda per quart (946 ml) of water to the bowl, and let the items soak for 10 minutes. Rinse and dry thoroughly with a soft cloth. Don't use this method to remove tarnish from hollow-handled silverware; use with caution on items that are held together with glue or cement, as the boiling water may loosen the adhesive.

Other Stains—Paints/Lacquers

NAIL POLISH

On clothing/washable fabric:

❦ Nail-polish stains may be permanent. Place the stain face down on a pad of paper towels, and apply non-oily nail-polish remover to the back of the spot (test first on a hidden part of the item; do not use on acetate fabrics). Change the pad under the spot frequently as it absorbs the polish and remover. Repeat until no more color comes out of the mark, which may be before the stain is entirely gone. Rinse with cool water and launder as usual.

On carpet:

❦ Act quickly to blot up as much of a spill as possible while it's still wet; use care to keep from spreading the stain further. Non-oily nail-polish remover is about the only option for dealing with this tough stain. Test it on a hidden part of your carpet first—if it doesn't take all the color out or eat away the fibers, proceed with caution on the stain itself. Use a cotton swab, eye dropper, or spoon to apply a minimal amount of nail-polish remover to the stain, and blot immediately with the corner of a soft white cloth or white paper towel. Use a lifting motion to avoid pressing the polish further into the fibers. Continue until all the stain is lifted. If the polish spill resists non-oily nail-polish remover, try full-strength acetone (available from beauticians' supply outlets)—but test on a hidden spot before applying to the stain. Once you've removed as much of the spill as possible, sponge the treated area with a mild solution of ¼ teaspoon (1.25 ml) of dishwashing liquid in ½ cup (120 ml) of water; blot, rinse with clear water, and blot dry. Use hydrogen peroxide to bleach any stain that remains. When finished, consider choosing a new, noncarpeted location for applying nail polish.

On tile or waxed floors:

🌿 Wait until the spill has started to solidify, then use a putty knife to scrape at the edge, and carefully peel up the spot. Wipe up smears of polish while still wet with a cloth or cotton ball moistened with non-oily nail-polish remover. Clean up with mild detergent solution.

PAINT SPATTERS, ON FINISHED WOOD:

🌿 Moisten old paint spots with linseed oil, and wait while the paint softens. Carefully scrape away spots. Make a paste of rottenstone and linseed oil, and rub over traces and smears; then wipe clean with a soft cloth, and polish as usual.

Spatters, on glass/windows:

🌿 Heat vinegar until it's hot (but not too hot to work with), and pour into a spray bottle. Spray freshly dried paint spatters, and wipe away.

🌿 Old paint spots may require harsher treatment: dab with turpentine, let soften, and scrape off with a

Be Particular About Paint Removal

In general, paint products are meant to be permanent once they've been applied to a surface and dried. Over the years, paint manufacturers have enhanced their products to make them longer-lasting and more durable. That's good news if you want the paint on the outside of your house to last for a long time, or when you have to clean painted walls inside your house. It can be bad news, however, if you're dealing with paint that's been spilled or spattered some-place where it isn't wanted. Most paints clean up relative-ly easily when they're wet. Removing dried paint requires a product-specific approach and often involves strong solvents. While general instructions for cleaning up common types of paint are provided here, you should consult the manufacturer of the specific paint formulation you're using to get the best possible recommendations for removal of spills and spatters.

putty knife (it's safer than a razor blade and serves the same purpose in this case).

🌿 Dab old paint spots with nail-polish remover, let soften for a few minutes, then wipe away with a cloth. Wash windows afterward to remove any residue.

PAINT (ACRYLIC)

On clothing/washable fabric:

🌿 Act fast to remove acrylic paint spatters and spills from fabric. Acrylic paint washes away easily with soap and water when it's wet but sets firmly once it has dried. Rinse fabric with cold water until no more color comes out of the stain. Put a pad of paper towels or cloth under the stain, and blot on isopropyl alcohol (test fabric for colorfastness) to saturate the stain. Blot with cotton balls or a cloth; change the padding under the stain as it becomes soaked with alcohol and paint residue. Launder in the hottest water that is safe for the fabric, using all-fabric bleach; rinse with warm water.

On carpet/upholstery:

🌿 Blot up as much of the stain as possible, taking care to avoid spreading it further. Dab isopropyl alcohol on the spot, and blot with clean cloths or white paper towels. Test for colorfastness in a hidden or inconspicuous spot before applying alcohol to carpet or upholstery.

PAINT (LATEX)

On clothing/washable fabric:

🌿 Blot up as much paint as possible with paper towels, taking care to avoid spreading the stain or forcing it into the fabric. Sponge or rinse the spot with luke-warm water to remove more paint and to keep the paint from drying. Lay the stain face down on a pad of paper towels or cloths, and sponge the back of the stain with a solution of 1 teaspoon (5 ml) of clear dishwashing liquid in 2 cups (475 ml) of warm water. Change the padding as it absorbs paint; continue sponging the stain until no more paint comes out of it. Launder right away in warm water, and let air dry.

On carpet:

❧ Blot paint spills immediately with paper towels, then sponge with cold water, rinsing your sponge or cloth frequently to avoid spreading the stain. Keep the spot wet, and continue until you've cleaned up as much paint as possible, then blot dry with clean cloths. Denatured alcohol may loosen dried latex paint, but it may also loosen the dyes in your carpet. Test first on an inconspicuous spot; if it doesn't harm the carpet, apply as little as necessary to remove the paint stain. Sponge with mild dishwashing liquid solution (¼ teaspoon [1.25 ml] in ½ cup [120 ml] of warm water), rinse, and blot dry.

On windows:

🍃 Rub paint spatters on windows with a clean eraser. If you have a typewriter eraser around the house, use its eraser end on the paint spots, then brush away the residue with the stiff bristles at the other end.

PAINT (GLOSS AND OIL-BASED)

On clothing/washable fabric:

🍃 Clean up as much paint as possible while it's still wet. After testing for colorfastness, dab turpentine on remaining spots and dried stains. Sponge with cold water and repeat until all paint is removed; laundering will set the paint in the fabric.

On carpet:

🍃 Blot up wet paint with paper towels, sponge with 1 teaspoon (5 ml) of clear dishwashing liquid in 2 cups (475 ml) of warm water, blot and repeat until the stain is lifted. Consult with the paint manufacturer for recommended solvents to remove dried or old spots. Use nail scissors to snip off the top of the pile to remove small stains.

On hands/skin:

🌿 Paint on your hands? Where are the gloves you should be wearing? Before you dry your skin out with paint thinner, try cleaning off oil paints with vegetable oil, then wash up with soap and water.

PAINT (WATERCOLOR)
On clothing/washable fabric:

🌿 Gently scrape and brush (dried paint) or rinse (wet paint) as much paint as possible from the surface. Soak for 30 minutes in a solution of ½ teaspoon (2.5 ml) of dishwashing liquid and 1 tablespoon (15 ml) of ammonia (don't use ammonia for silk or wool fabrics) in 1 quart (946 ml) of warm water. Rinse with clear water, and soak for 1 hour in 1 quart

A Few "Stains" You Can't Solve

Sometimes a mark on a surface isn't really a mark on the surface—it's a mark *in* the surface. No matter how good you are at stain removal, there's little you can do when what appears to be a stain turns out to be the result of physical wear and tear. Damage caused by abrasion, burns, cuts, or tears requires more than successful stain treatment.

In such cases, the best you can hope for is to mitigate the appearance of the damage: Use crayons to touch up faded spots or abrasions on wallpaper; fill gouges in wood with wood putty and stain or paint to match; touch up dings in painted walls; lightly sand away minor cuts in countertops. Holes in fabric may be patched (in the knees of jeans, perhaps), enjoyed as part of a garment's style (again, as in jeans), or enough reason to discard the garment. Fraying around collars and cuffs may appear to be stains, but actually may be damage to the fibers. Take comfort in knowing that nothing lasts forever, and consign irreparable garments to the rag bag or your dirty-job wardrobe.

(946 ml) of warm water with 1 tablespoon (15 ml) of white vinegar added. Rinse again; launder with all-fabric bleach.

On carpet:

🌿 Soak up wet spills with paper towels; brush/ vacuum dried residues to remove as much as possible. Blot remaining spot with a sponge dipped in isopropyl alcohol (test for colorfastness first), continuing until no more color comes out of the spot. Blot with mild dishwashing liquid solution (¼ teaspoon [1.25 ml] in ½ cup [120 ml] of warm water) to remove remaining residue; rinse and blot with clear water, then blot dry with clean cloths.

Other Stains—Physical Damage

BLEACH

On clothing/fabric:

🌿 Dilute with cool water, taking care to avoid spreading the bleach but rinsing it out as thoroughly as you can.

❦ If a lightened area remains where the bleach removed dye from the fabric, consider bleaching the entire garment to even the color. Try this only on fabrics that are labeled for chlorine bleach use and use ¼ cup (60 ml) of liquid bleach in a gallon of lukewarm water. Soak the garment for up to 30 minutes, then rinse in cool water. If a care label prohibits chlorine bleach use, try an oxygen bleach product, and follow the label directions.

❦ Ultimately, camouflage may be your only option. If you've stained a garment in an inconspicuous place, you may be able to color the spot well enough to blend in with the rest of the fabric. Visit an art supply store, and check out the selection of permanent markers. If possible, take the fabric with you to find the best color match. Read the label on the markers to see if they're safe for use on the fabric you wish to color. Then, carefully dab the marker on the spot, taking care to apply only small amounts of ink to the bleached area of the garment. Let it dry, then evaluate the results. If the treated spot is unnoticeable, you've saved your garment; if it stands out even more than before, you have a new item to wear the next time you clean the toilet.

The Anti-Stain

Unlike most spills, bleach takes the color out of things instead of putting an unwanted color on them. Liquid chlorine bleach (sodium hypochlorite) can be useful for removing stains from white cotton and linen fabrics (and some synthetics), but only if a fabric care label indicates it is safe for use. Even then, its use can weaken fabric fibers so they wear out sooner than they normally would, especially if the bleach stays on the fabric too long or is not rinsed out thoroughly. When used with care, mild bleaching agents such as hydrogen peroxide (the type sold in drugstores for antiseptic use) and oxygen laundry products can help you remove stains. But

BURN MARKS (*SEE ALSO* SCORCH MARKS, PAGE 235)

On carpet:

🌿 Use fine-grade sandpaper to rub away mildly scorched fibers, or trim off minor damage with nail scissors. Use a matching remnant to patch large burned spots, or place an end table or floor lamp over them.

what can you do when you have an unintended encounter with a potent bleach product, like toilet bowl cleaner or undiluted chlorine bleach?

If you've sloshed a bit of chlorine bleach on your clothing or dripped toilet bowl cleaner on the rug, you've seen how easily these products take the color out of things. The difficult-to-impossible part is restoring the color once it's been bleached out. Here's where you have to weigh the value of the item that's been spotted. Is it clothing or a bathroom rug that you can replace or do without? Or is it a favorite item or irreplaceable? If it's worth your while, seek professional help for repairing or replacing carpeting or flooring that's been damaged by bleaching agents, or for treating spots on dry-clean-only fabrics (don't expect miracles).

On finished wood:

❦ Use furniture polish or (in a pinch) mayonnaise to treat light burn marks. Apply it to the mark, and let it set for 15–30 minutes, then wipe it off with a soft cloth.

❦ Mix a paste of rottenstone or powdered pumice with linseed oil or vegetable oil, and rub it over the burned spot, working with the grain of the wood. If you don't have rottenstone, use cigarette or wood ashes with the oil to make a paste. Moisten a rag with linseed oil, and use it to wipe away the paste, then polish with a clean cloth.

On brick or stone:

❦ Use a stiff brush to scrub burned marks with clear water. Follow by sponging white vinegar over the marks, then rinse thoroughly with fresh water.

On vinyl flooring:

❦ Remove burn marks by rubbing gently with fine-grade sandpaper.

MILDEW

On clothing/washable fabric:

❦ For light-colored fabrics, apply a paste of lemon juice and salt to stains. Set the item in sunlight to bleach, then rinse with clear water, and launder as usual.

❦ Make a paste by moistening borax with water or liquid detergent, and apply to the stain. Let the paste dry, brush it off, and launder as usual, adding borax to your normal detergent in the washer.

On bathroom grout:

❦ Rub out stains with a dry typewriter eraser as soon as you notice them. For bigger jobs, scrub with baking soda paste (3 parts baking soda to 1 part water), and rinse well.

❧ Tough stains may require harsher treatments: Brush on bleach solution (¼ cup [60 ml] of chlorine bleach in 1 quart [946 ml] of warm water), scrub, and rinse. Or make a paste by moistening baking soda with chlorine bleach, brush onto grout, and let dry before rinsing with clear water. Always ventilate your work area when using chlorine bleach, and be sure to rinse treated surfaces thoroughly. Be careful if you're using bleach near carpets, curtains, towels, or other fabrics—strong bleach fumes can cause colors to fade. Do not mix other household cleansers with bleach; some combinations (ammonia, most notably) create toxic fumes.

❧ If you're not using bleach, make a solution of 1 teaspoon ammonia, ¼ cup (60 ml) of hydrogen peroxide, and ¾ cup (175 ml) of water. Scrub stains with the solution, and let it soak in for several minutes before rinsing with clear water. Repeat as needed to remove stains.

On shower curtains:

❧ Make a habit of washing your shower curtain liner every couple of months, and mildew buildup will never become a problem. Wash the liner with several light-colored towels (old ones, useful for this purpose and for blotting and padding during stain-removal efforts). The towels will help to "scrub" mildew and soap scum off the liner. To your usual liquid laundry detergent, add 1 cup white vinegar, and wash in warm water. Hang the liner back on the rod after laundering.

On most household surfaces:

❧ Mix 2 teaspoons (28 ml) of tea tree oil (available at health food stores) with 2 cups (475 ml) of water, and apply with a spray bottle to places where mildew has formed. Leave on the surface; rinsing is unnecessary.

On upholstery:

❧ Dip a cut lemon half in salt, and rub over the stain; place the item in the sun to dry. Use a stiff brush to brush away the mildew, then sponge with ¼ teaspoon (1.25 ml) of clear dishwashing liquid in ½ cup (120 ml) of warm water with a few drops of ammonia added. Rinse and blot dry.

❧ Treat persistent stains with a solution of equal parts denatured alcohol in water (test for colorfastness on a hidden location before applying). Vacuum the spot first, then sponge on the alcohol solution, and blot thoroughly.

On leather:

❧ Coat mildew with petroleum jelly, and leave on for several hours before wiping off with a soft cloth.

❧ Or sponge with equal parts isopropyl or denatured alcohol and water, wipe dry with a clean cloth, and apply an appropriate leather dressing.

On books:

❧ Sprinkle cornstarch over mildew spots, and let set for a few days. Brush away cornstarch and mildew. Store books where moisture is not a concern.

MYSTERY STAINS AND MARKS

On wallpaper:

❧ Remove the crust from a piece of white bread and wad the bread into a ball. Gently rub it over dirty spots on wallpaper.

On walls:

❧ Rub stray marks with an art gum eraser kept solely for this purpose. Dip a moistened cloth or sponge in baking soda, and rub over spots that resist your eraser. Plain white toothpaste (not gel) also works well and is easier to apply to vertical surfaces. Wipe away residue with a damp sponge.

On clothing/washable fabric:

🌿 Go easy on unidentified stains: sponge liberally with club soda. It might remove the spot, and it's unlikely to set it. If you have to proceed further, try to figure out what you're dealing with. A mild solution of dishwashing liquid (¼ teaspoon [1.25 ml] to ½ cup [120 ml] of tepid water) is a good, safe laundry pretreatment for stains.

On carpet:

🌿 Pour on club soda, and blot with clean white cloths or paper towels.

🌿 Add 2 tablespoons (28 g) of salt to ½ cup (120 ml) of white vinegar, and blot onto stains. Let dry, then vacuum up any residue.

🌿 Or add 2 tablespoons (28 g) of borax to the salt and vinegar mix above, and rub onto heavy stains. Allow to dry, then vacuum up residue.

SCORCH MARKS (*SEE ALSO* BURN MARKS, PAGE 227)

On clothing/washable fabric:

❧ Treat the stain with liquid detergent before washing in hot water with chlorine bleach. If the fabric care label forbids the use of chlorine bleach, dab the mark with a cloth dipped in hydrogen peroxide with a few drops of ammonia added, then launder in the hottest water safe for the fabric. If the stain persists, rub it lightly with fine-grade steel wool, and reapply hydrogen peroxide; this may cause the stain to fade but at the risk of damaging the fabric and creating a fuzzy spot.

On linen and cotton:

❧ Moisten a cloth with peroxide and place it over the scorch mark; press with a warm iron.

On linen:

🌿 Rub the stain with the cut side of an onion and soak in cold water.

Leave the Mysteries to Sherlock Holmes

Fans of the board game Clue may enjoy a good mystery, but mystery stains aren't nearly as much fun as a family-friendly who-dunnit. The best solution for mystery stains is to avoid encountering them: Treat spills when they happen so you know what you're dealing with and train (the hardest part of all) family members to report—and treat—spots and stains as soon as possible. Week-old mystery stains that have been "cured" in the bottom of a hamper are much harder to remove than when they were fresh.

If your avoidance techniques fail, and you're faced with a laundry-day mystery stain, use all the clues available to you to solve it before you treat or toss it in the washing machine. For garments, start with "who-stained-it?"—the laundry room version of who-dunnit. What has the garment's owner been doing? Where has that

On upholstery:

❦ Combine glycerin and warm water in equal parts and apply to light scorch marks; let set for 2 hours; rinse

person been? What do they commonly eat or drink? However, don't count on interrogation to reveal the nature of a stain—family members can be notoriously unreliable about remembering what they got on their clothing and when/where they got it.

Next look at the color, texture, and condition of the stain. Match it against your mental database of known foods, drinks, and activities. Recent participation in a pie-eating contest? Might be a fruit stain. Is it dark and smooth and soaked in? Probably grease or oil with soil added to the mix. Does it have

that "old fraternity house" aroma? Most likely a beer spill.

Take a similar tack when examining mystery stains on floors and upholstery, looking at the color and consistency of a spot to help identify its origins. Consider: What is the room commonly used for? Who sat there last? You may find yourself examining the shoes of everyone in the household to see who stepped in what.

As with all stains, patience is the key to making mystery stains disappear. If you can solve the mystery, chances are much better that you can dissolve the stain.

with clear water, and blot dry with clean cloths. Add 1 tablespoon (15 g) of borax to 2 cups (475 ml) of warm water, and sponge onto more severe scorch damage. Rinse and blot dry.

SCUFF/SKID MARKS
On wood flooring:
❦ Dab a small amount of vegetable oil on marks and rub lightly with very fine-grade steel wool (No. 0000) until the marks are removed. Wipe up any residue with a soft cloth.

On vinyl and other "hard" flooring:
❦ Rub away marks with a clean eraser. If erasing doesn't do the job, use a damp cloth to rub a little white toothpaste (not gel) or baking soda on the spots; wipe clean with a soft cloth or damp sponge when the marks are gone. Carefully rub persistent scuff marks with dry fine-grade steel wool (No. 00); wipe clean with a soft, damp cloth.

WATER STAINS/MARKS

On finished wood:

🌿 Apply patience, for at least a day or two, when failure to use a coaster leaves a whitish ring on a table top. As the moisture evaporates, the mark may disappear.

🌿 If the spot fails to leave on its own, coat it with mayonnaise, and leave it overnight; wipe away the mayonnaise with a clean, dry cloth, and clean and polish as usual.

🌿 If a water mark lingers on after a coating of mayonnaise, mix a mildly abrasive paste by combining ashes (cigarette or fireplace) or rottenstone with olive oil, vegetable oil, mayonnaise, linseed oil, or petroleum jelly. You can also use a paste-type furniture wax and very fine-grade steel wool (No. 0000), or white, non-gel toothpaste (rub on with a damp cloth). Rub gently over the spot with a soft cloth, working with the

Get Used to Old Stains

The longer a stain stays on a surface, the more likely it is to "set" or become a permanent part of that surface. Depending on what caused the stain, exposure to heat, sunlight, cleansers, water, acids, alkalines, or even the natural oils found on your skin may help to cement its position. Furthermore, old stains are usually mystery stains, and their age often precludes any chance of figuring out what caused them. Finally, many staining agents are virtual dirt magnets. An old stain may be a combination of the original stain material plus any dirt that has stuck to it in the weeks, months, or perhaps years since the stain occurred. Any attempt at removal will have to work on the dirt that's been piling on, as well as the original stain. Ultimately, that can be a tall order.

If you're desperate to salvage an article that bears a long-standing stain, there are a few methods to try. For garments, start by soaking in cool water. The longer you can soak something, the better—at least 30 minutes up to several hours. Increase the effectiveness of soaking by using salt water, or by adding white vinegar (no more than ½ cup [120 ml] per 2 quarts [1.8 L] water; it may weaken cotton, rayon, acetate, and silk) or ammonia (1-2 tablespoons [15-28 ml] per 2 quarts [1.8 L] water; don't use for silk or wool fabric) to the water. After soaking, rinse in clear water, sponge the stain with mild dishwashing liquid solution, and launder in the warmest water recommended for the fabric.

Because it absorbs water, glycerin is often recommended for "loosening" stains that have dried, improving the chances that they can be flushed out of fibers with the same cleaning solutions you'd use on fresh stains. Work glycerin into an old stain, and let it set for several hours before sponging with a mild detergent solution and laundering or spot cleaning (depending on the surface).

Another good bet for treating old stains is to bleach them so they're less visible. Hydrogen peroxide (the 3-percent solution used for household first aid) is a gentle, safe bleaching agent. Test for colorfastness on a hidden spot before applying it to a visible part of the item you want to treat—it can take the color out of fabrics and carpet. Dab on the stain at full strength; if it appears to lighten the stain, continue applying until the spot is sufficiently diminished.

grain of the wood, and leave the paste in place for a few minutes. Avoid the temptation to really scrub at the spot; you may scratch the wood. Wipe away the paste with a clean, soft cloth; once the mark is gone and the spot is dry, wax or polish as usual.

Inside a vase, from stale flower water:

❧ Fill the vase halfway with crushed ice, and pour in white vinegar to cover the ice and fill the vase. Shake/swirl the ice and vinegar in the vase and let set overnight. Empty and rinse with clear water.

On silk/nonwashable fabric:

❧ Use a kettle of boiling water to get rid of watermarks on silk. Hold a kettle of boiling water so the steam from the spout passes over the spot; continue until the mark is gone. Keep your fingers clear of the steam to avoid burns.

On leather:

◉ Wipe with a damp sponge and let dry.

◉ Use a suede-cleaning block or a clean pencil eraser to gently rub water marks on suede. As the nap regains its shape, the water marks will all but disappear.

RESOURCES

Additional Stain-Removal Resources

THERE ARE A NUMBER of useful books that address general cleaning techniques along with stain removal. Those listed here are especially comprehensive. At your local library or at any used-book sale, you may find treasure troves of "old" cleaning books. Many of them are fun to read for their insights into housekeeping history, and they may also include tried-and-true cleaning and stain-removal instructions that have been passed down through generations of housekeepers. Old cleaning books often hold household remedies you can still use today, but they may also include information that is outdated because of products that are no longer available, changes to product formulas, changes to fabric content/finishes/dyes, or changes in our knowledge of what is safe for our health and the health of our environment. If you look back far enough, you'll find cleaning recommendations that are very natural, simply because there weren't many cleaning chemicals widely available. But you may also find recommendations for practices that are no longer advisable because we now know that they present unnecessary or unacceptable health and/or environmental risks.

By contrast, information on websites is bound to be more up-to-date, simply by virtue of that medium's much more recent arrival on the information scene. The vast majority of cleaning information available on the Internet is provided by manufacturers of cleaning products or manufacturers of products that may require cleaning. While you're likely to find very specific information on the manufacturer's Web site about using (or cleaning up) a particular product successfully, it's useful to remember that their goal is to sell their product. Caveat emptor, as they say.

I have found the following resources to be useful; you may, too, if you are looking for cleaning guidance beyond the scope of this book. Inclusion on this list does not imply endorsement.

Books

Aslett, Don. *Don Aslett's Stain-Buster's Bible: The Complete Guide to Spot Removal.* Pocatello, Idaho: Marshall Creek Press, 2002.

Bond, Annie Berthold. *Better Basics for the Home.* New York, New York: Three Rivers Press, 1999.

Bredenberg, Jeff. *Clean It Fast, Clean It Right.* Emmaus, PA: Rodale Press, Inc., 1998.

Cobb, Linda. *Talking Dirty with the Queen of Clean®,* Second Edition. New York, New York: Pocket Books, a division of Simon & Schuster, Inc., 2004.

Consumer Reports Books. *How to Clean and Care for Practically Anything.* Yonkers, NY: Consumer Union of United States, Inc., 2002.

Smallin, Donna. *Cleaning Plain & Simple.* North Adams, MA: Storey Publishing, 2006.

Websites

www.housekeepingchannel.com
A compilation of tips and resources for housekeeping, including articles, reviews, and forums where members can post housekeeping questions. Register on the site for free membership.

www.laundry101.com
Web site of The Soap and Detergent Association; includes downloadable fact sheets on cleaning topics for all areas of the home.

www.thelaundrybasket.com
Tips on using washing soda, from Church & Dwight Co., Inc., makers of Arm & Hammer Super Washing Soda.

www.naturallyyoursclean.com
Source of environmentally safe cleaning products, including natural solvent and enzyme products.

www.purex.com
Downloadable booklet of tips on using borax from The Dial Corporation, makers of 20 Mule Team® Borax; site also features an "interactive stain guide."

www.queenofclean.com
Cleaning tips, recommended products, books, and videos from The Queen of Clean Linda Cobb; paid membership in the "Castle Club" gives access to entire library of cleaning tips and includes a monthly e-mail newsletter.

www.rederase.com

Tips on use of Red Erase Red Stain Remover from makers Evergreen Labs, Inc.; includes product reviews and testimonials from users.

www.wineaway.com

Tips on use of Wine Away Red Wine Stain Remover from makers Evergreen Labs, Inc.; includes product reviews and testimonials from users.

Index

tools, 39–57
"toughing it out," 10–12, 33
treatments, 39–57
Tripoli. See rottenstone
types of stains, 9

U

underside, treating from the, 29
unsolvable stains, 223
urine, 76–79, 81, 82

V

vegetable oil, 52
ventilation, 19
vinegar, 53
vomit, pet, 78
vomit stains, 83–84

W

washable marker, 119–121
washing soda
    (sodium carbonate), 59–60
water stains/marks, 239, 242–243
wax, candle, 178–181
WD-40, 53
wet spills, 25–26
wine, 124–128, 137
Wine Away, 170–171
wool, 57

Y

yogurt, 83